GOSPEL BOOTCAMP

How God Practically Shapes and Supports
the Lives of Believers Through the Good News:

Highlights from Paul's Letter to the Romans

JEREMY WEIMER

WestBow Press
A DIVISION OF THOMAS NELSON
& ZONDERVAN

Copyright © 2018 Jeremy Weimer.

All rights reserved. No part of this book may be used or reproduced by any means, graphic, electronic, or mechanical, including photocopying, recording, taping or by any information storage retrieval system without the written permission of the author except in the case of brief quotations embodied in critical articles and reviews.

This book is a work of non-fiction. Unless otherwise noted, the author and the publisher make no explicit guarantees as to the accuracy of the information contained in this book and in some cases, names of people and places have been altered to protect their privacy.

WestBow Press books may be ordered through booksellers or by contacting:

WestBow Press
A Division of Thomas Nelson & Zondervan
1663 Liberty Drive
Bloomington, IN 47403
www.westbowpress.com
1 (866) 928-1240

Because of the dynamic nature of the Internet, any web addresses or links contained in this book may have changed since publication and may no longer be valid. The views expressed in this work are solely those of the author and do not necessarily reflect the views of the publisher, and the publisher hereby disclaims any responsibility for them.

Any people depicted in stock imagery provided by Thinkstock are models, and such images are being used for illustrative purposes only.
Certain stock imagery © Thinkstock.

Unless otherwise stated, scripture quotations taken from the New American Standard Bible® (NASB), Copyright © 1960, 1962, 1963, 1968, 1971, 1972, 1973, 1975, 1977, 1995 by The Lockman Foundation Used by permission. www.Lockman.org

Scripture quotations marked (NIV) are taken from the Holy Bible, New International Version®, NIV®. Copyright © 1973, 1978, 1984, 2011 by Biblica, Inc.™ Used by permission of Zondervan. All rights reserved worldwide. www.zondervan.com
The "NIV" and "New International Version" are trademarks registered in the United States Patent and Trademark Office by Biblica, Inc.™

ISBN: 978-1-9736-1229-2 (sc)
ISBN: 978-1-9736-1230-8 (hc)
ISBN: 978-1-9736-1228-5 (e)

Library of Congress Control Number: 2017919452

Print information available on the last page.

WestBow Press rev. date: 2/8/2018

This Book Is Dedicated To:

Melissa, my wife

Beth, my daughter

Daniel, my son

> Thank you for being so patient with me, especially in the times when it was very difficult to see Christ in me. He shines brightly in you!

Fred and Liz, my parents

> I saw this Truth in your lives long before I ever saw it in Scripture or in the heart of God.

Chris, my brother

> He left an incredible legacy. We had the same message, but his actions will echo louder and longer than my words ever will.

Acknowledgments:

Brent, Marc, Lee, Wayne, Jervey

> You read though the very first version of this book with me—back when "boot camp" was even more challenging to survive! I will be forever grateful for your encouragement and guidance.

TRANSLATION FOR SCRIPTURE REFERENCES:

All scriptures cited are from the New American Standard Bible (NASB) translation, unless otherwise noted.

INTRODUCTION
Gospel Boot Camp

"...I am not ashamed of the gospel,
for it is the power of God for salvation to everyone who believes...
For in it the righteousness of God is revealed, from faith to faith;
As it is written, 'but the righteous will live by faith'"
—Romans 1:16-17

Basic Training

When the military recruits a new soldier, where do they send them first? The front lines? Recon? Strategic planning? Of course not. They send the new recruit to boot camp. Basic Training is the first step to becoming a successful soldier. Before the experienced military officers can expect a new recruit to:

- perform well under pressure
- think like a soldier
- have the self-control and discipline a soldier needs
- and consistently act like a soldier

The officers know the soldier's whole frame of reference for life must be broken down and reshaped. Then, the new recruit needs some time to develop experience working with the new "soldier" mindset.

I intend for this short book to be Christian boot camp for your mind, soul, and heart—Basic Training for a life of faith. It is for anyone who wants to live in relationship with Jesus Christ and successfully fight the good fight of faith. My heart aches for the millions of Christians in the world today who are on the battle lines for Christ, but they have never received the most basic instructions on how their faith really works. My goal is not to give you answers to all your questions about Christianity, theology, doctrine, and practical application in all life areas. This simple book is a basic framework for evaluating life, God, and yourself as a Christian. This is a foundational perspective guide to help you get your bearings as a believer and identify when you may be veering from the path. I'm not giving you all the *fish* you will need to eat for the rest of your life; I ask God to use these words to *teach you how to fish* yourself. I pray that this book will encourage and support you so you can walk in the wisdom of God, while identifying falsehood and deception that could sabotage your trust in Him.

WHY PAUL AND WHY ROMANS?

Paul's letter to the Romans is the perfect book to chart this course for us for two reasons:

First, Paul is the apostle entrusted with the responsibility of explaining the gospel to those who were not raised with a Jewish, or Bible-believing worldview. Aside from Christ Himself, no one else was given as much Godly insight and supernatural capacity to communicate the basics of Christianity to those who don't yet understand how the gospel works.[1]

Second, Romans is unique among Paul's letters. All his other letters are written to believers in churches that he had planted himself, or at least in churches where Paul had personally discipled those who planted the

---

[1] Galatians 2:7-9-- The 1st century church apostles in Jerusalem recognized that Paul had been entrusted in a unique way by the grace of God to go to the Gentiles with the message of the gospel.

church.[2] Paul knew the readers of all of his other letters had already been taught the gospel basics, so he was just filling in the details and reminding the other churches of areas where they still needed to grow. The church in Rome was different. Paul had not been there, and he had only a few connections in the church. He was unsure if they had all the "essentials" to shape the framework for their lives as believers. So, **in Romans, he lays out all the basics in careful detail**. This is exactly what I hope to do for you.

One challenge for us in today's culture is that Paul's writings are complex and loaded with details meant for an audience that lived about 2,000 years ago. It's all great information, but it's also easy to *lose the forest for the trees*. So often the main thing he is saying gets lost in his explanation of the details. Have you ever wished that the writers of the Bible would have had highlighters, or the ability to underline, or write in bold—*something* to help us identify the key verses? **In this book I am picking the highlight verses and carefully explaining them in today's language**. Should I have called the book SportsCenter for Christianity? Or maybe the Gospel's Slow-Mo highlight reel? The church's Top-10?

Why Take Input From Me?

I may not have the academic or full-time ministry accolades that other Christian writers have, but I have devoted the last eighteen years of my life to pursuing a relationship with God by boldly believing that what God's Word says is true. To say the experience has been "profound" would be an understatement. I have studied the Bible and learned to live it genuinely, though imperfectly, through the trials of life. God has used my family to teach me the most, and I have invested in others through small group ministry. God has shown me so much through His Word, and I believe He has done that, in part, because He wants me to encourage you. He has given me a passion to see Christians grow to maturity in

---

[2] If I'm not mistaken, I believe Colossians is the only other letter of Paul that was written primarily to people Paul had not met; and he trained Epaphras, who taught the gospel to the church in Colossae.

their faith and to fulfill their eternal purpose—to "Be all they can be" in the sight of God.

Disclaimer and Warning

Please don't expect to like everything I say. It's boot camp! This is supposed to be challenging. Some of the material may be awkward or upsetting because I am intentionally questioning common misconceptions within Christian thinking. Writing a book like this is so delicate; it's like walking through a minefield. I would be surprised if I did not touch on at least a few areas that disturb the way you have always thought about your faith. Central to this book is this questioning process:

> Is what you believe really based in the Bible, or has it come from somewhere else? Most of your faith is probably right out of Scripture; some of it probably is not. Let's make sure the essentials you are building your life on are grounded in God's eternal and inspired Word.

I am convinced that this process will be of tremendous benefit to your growth as a follower of Christ. Going to the gym challenges your muscles; it often causes soreness and fatigue at first. But the challenge is critical to making the muscles stronger. Faith and relationship with God work the same way: being challenged is very healthy for us.

This is not a long book, but it is meant to be digested slowly. My intent is for my readers to read one chapter at a time, possibly one per week with the study guide. One of my goals is that you will read the chapter from this book and then be able to go back and read the chapter from Romans with greater clarity and understanding. My hope and prayer is that this book will be a helpful and delightful resource to you personally—to the extent that you will look forward to sharing it with others to encourage them in their faith.

I think this could be an excellent book for a church small group. If I only get your attention for one sitting... I'll take it! By all means, read the whole book. But I do think you will get a greater blessing if you *chew it slowly*. This isn't a drive-thru/quick-snack type of book; it's a steak. Take your time and savor the wisdom, power, and glorious heart of God that the gospel so beautifully proclaims!

CONTENTS

INTRODUCTION	Gospel Boot Camp	vii
CHAPTER 1	Where Did All The Mess Come From?	1
CHAPTER 2	What Do I Do Next—Now That I Am A Christian?	21
CHAPTER 3	How Does The Process Work?	29
CHAPTER 4	What Does God See?	41
CHAPTER 5	What Should I Expect Next?	51
CHAPTER 6	What Are We Supposed To Do?	59
CHAPTER 7	How Could This Be True Of Me?	69
CHAPTER 8	Can We Have A Summary Of The "Good" News?	79
CHAPTER 9	What Should My Goal And Strategy Be?	87
CHAPTER 10	What Is The Heart Behind It All?	93
APPENDIX	The Law Of 1st Mention Of Mankind	101

ROMANS OUTLINE   GOSPEL BOOT CAMP OUTLINE

Introduction (1:1-17)   Introduction

The REJECTION of the Righteousness of God (1:18 – 3:20)

Romans 1	Ch. 1	Where did all the mess come from?
Romans 2	Ch. 2	What do I do Next?

The REVELATION of the Righteousness of God (3:21 – 8:39)

Romans 3	Ch. 3	How does the Process work?
Romans 4	Ch. 4	What does God See?
Romans 5	Ch. 5	What should I Expect next?
Romans 6	Ch. 6	What are we supposed to **Do**?
Romans 7	Ch. 7	How could this be true of Me?
Romans 8	Ch. 8	Can we have a Summary?

The RESISTANCE to and RESTORATION of the Righteousness of God (9:1 – 11:36)

                 (A project for another book)

The REFLECTION of the Righteousness of God (12:1 – 15:13)

Romans 12	Ch. 9	What should my goal and strategy be?
Romans 13-15	Ch. 10	What is the heart behind it all?

Closing and personal Greetings (15:14 – 16:31)

                 Appendix – Law of first mention of man (Genesis 1-3)

CHAPTER 1

WHERE DID ALL THE MESS COME FROM?
THE STRONG INFLUENCE OF PERCEPTION AND DECEPTION

"...people, who suppress the truth" - Romans 1:18

HAVE YOU WONDERED WHERE AND WHY?

Do you see things happening in the world around you that are disturbing? For me, the news is painful to watch. My social media news feeds aren't safe either. I'll spare you statistics because they are everywhere, but I am sure you could make a long list of troubling issues in no time at all. Our world has big issues, so does our country, along with our communities, and our families.

Where did all the mess come from? Why is it so prevalent? For 2,000+ years the church has answered: "Because of sin." I agree, but I am not confident that we have a very good understanding of what that means. It seems that most people think of sin as simply "bad choices" and "evil things that people do." That is sin, but sin is not that simple. Why are people making bad choices everywhere, and why do so few seem to be able to consistently make good ones? Something is not right in mankind. Did God make us flawed? If not, how did we become flawed?

How Does Paul Explain The Source Of All The Mess?

In Romans 1:16-32, Paul explains the answer in careful detail. I encourage you to take the time to look up all of the scripture references in this book. Try to appreciate them all in their context. But this one is particularly important because it lays out the foundation of Paul's worldview, his gospel presentation, and his ministry.[3]

I will summarize Paul's explanation this way:

> Since the beginning, people have made sinful choices **because** we feel crazy feelings and desire sinful things.[4] We feel and desire those corrupt things **because** we are thinking corrupted thoughts.[5] And finally we get back to the root of the problem, which is the focus of this chapter:
>
>> Our thinking, feelings, desires, and consequently our actions are all tainted **because** our perception of God and relationship with Him are not right.

The Man On The Frozen Lake

I find this concept about perception influencing people's thoughts, feelings, desires, and choices easiest to understand in story form:

> Many years ago, before mobile phones, or WIFI, or Amazon prime delivery, a man and his wife lived in a secluded cabin in Canada. Their cabin was on an island, surrounded by a lake. They could see

---

[3] I am convinced that Christians worldwide would be able to appreciate what Christ has done for them and walk in the practical power of the gospel much more effectively if we understood in greater depth the starting point that Paul lays out here in Romans 1.

[4] Our hearts were darkened and given over to impurity [vs 21, 24], our passions degraded [vs 26]

[5] We suppressed the truth of God and exchanged it for a lie [vs 18, 25], given over to a depraved mind [vs 28]).

a small town in the distance from the cabin, but could only get to the town by boat.

One winter, the man's wife became very ill, and he knew that her life depended on him getting to town for medicine. Unfortunately, the lake was frozen and the boat was useless. The man's only option would be to walk across the frozen lake. But he had no idea if the ice could support him.

He began to worry about the thickness of the ice. Would he fall through? Or worse, would it be strong enough to support him only until he got out in the middle where the water would be deep when he broke through? He dreaded the prospect of walking across and possibly freezing to death! Fear gripped him, and his hands began to sweat, even though it was bitterly cold. He decided to wait another day and reevaluate his wife's condition tomorrow.

The next day her condition had worsened, and he knew he could wait no longer. But he regretted his decision to wait because that day was a sunny day. It was still freezing outside, but the thought of the sun's rays shining on the ice all day made him even more nervous than the day before. Finally, he made himself step out on the frozen surface.

His mind was consumed with concern over the strength and reliability of the frozen lake beneath him. About 50 feet out from the shore he couldn't make himself walk anymore. He was down on his hands and knees crawling, trying desperately to spread his weight out over a larger area. He experienced a wide range of emotions:

- Anxiety over his predicament
- Anger at God for putting him in this situation
- Regret for choosing such a secluded home
- Desperate "if-only" bargaining with God for his life

- Bitterness at his wife for going outside without her coat and getting sick in the first place!

Then, among the noise of his own thoughts, he heard a sound. It must have been the ice cracking, he thought. "I'm done for!" echoed in his mind. He lay down flat on the ice. He didn't even move. The noise grew louder, though muffled through his many layers of clothing. It didn't sound like ice cracking, but he knew it had to be bad.

Then a team of horses, pulling a sled, raced by him on the ice… They glided across the ice fearlessly from the direction of his cabin toward the town. He quickly realized the foolishness of his fears; the ice was strong enough to support a team of horses! After that, he got up from the ice and ran the rest of the way across the lake to get the medicine for his wife.

Can you see how the man's perception that the ice "might not be strong enough" had such a huge impact on his thoughts, feelings, desires, and actions? He did *not* want to go out on that lake! But it was perfectly safe. He put off doing the right thing longer than he should have, and he was miserable even when he did go forward. All the issues resulted from his misperception about the stability of the ice. The Word of God teaches us that, in the same way, **our perception of life, particularly our concept of God, directly influences everything else in our heart, mind, and emotions.**

Picture A Plant—What Perception Produces

Understanding the impact of perception on the human soul has dramatically changed how I live my life and how I face challenges every day. I find it very helpful to think of sin in myself, and in people in general, like a plant growing in soil. **Sin has a Root, Shoot, and Fruit**:

ROOT (the source and cause of sin): Deception, false perceptions and beliefs (especially about God)

    Romans 1: 18-23, 25

SHOOT (the motivation and power of sin): Corrupt desires and feelings, godless ways of thinking

    Romans 1: 21-24, 26-27

FRUIT (the results and fulfillment of sin): Ungodly actions and choices

    Romans 1: 28-32

The practical implications of these observations are powerful. When I notice "bad fruit," or I want to see more "good fruit" in my life, I don't simply try to stop doing the bad stuff and start doing something different. I talk to God about it. I ask Him to show me what I'm not seeing and where bad assumptions are clouding my perception. When I am wrestling to do what He says is right, I ask Him to help me see why I am reluctant to do what I know He will reward me for.

When it comes to church and spiritual things, most people are trying to *get the weeds out of their yard by mowing the grass*. Simply trying to "stop sinning" will not be successful long-term. Try a different approach. Changing our thinking habits, being more aware of our feelings, and recognizing our own harmful desires are great steps in the right direction. But until we really go deep with God in prayer, until we allow Him to transform the way we see Him and the world around us through His Word, our victory over sin will be limited. Authentic, lasting change happens when we stop being "people who suppress the Truth," and become those who embrace the Truth—Jesus Christ.

Does it seem like I am minimizing the importance of sinful choices? That is not my intent, nor do I believe our decisions are insignificant. What we *choose* to say reinforces our perception; and when we *choose* to act in sin the seed of bad fruit is planted in the soil of our lives again. The fruit of sinful choices will multiply the root and shoot of sin within us; so those choices are crucial. But my goal in this chapter has been to improve our awareness of what Paul explains in Romans 1:

> Bad choices are not the root of the problem; the root is bad perception—especially false perception of God.

A Challenge In Conclusion

My challenge to you for this chapter is to **pray for God to help you be aware of the battle that is raging for your perception**. I pray that the chapter 1 study guide will give you greater insight into Paul's explanation of the dynamics of sin. Since the beginning with Adam and Eve, the "father of lies" has been using deception to dominate our perception. This falsehood is the source where "the mess" came from. With his schemes of lies the enemy afflicts the hearts and minds of people worldwide, leading us to consider, desire, and choose the insane things that we see on the news.

As you learn to walk closely with God—to see things like Him and think like Him—you will experience amazing freedom from the corruption of sin. God promises peace, even in difficult situations; knowing how to fight the battle for perception is an essential skill for walking in that peace and freedom.

Don't be like the foolish man cowering on the ice. Ask God to show you that He is a solid foundation; you can trust His faithfulness and "walk on water" without fear.

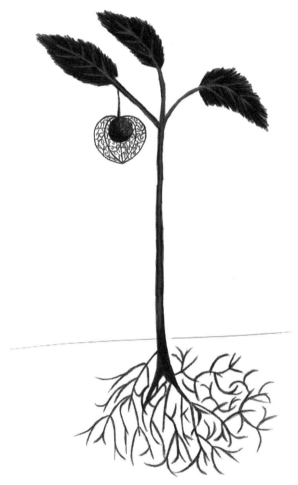

*Sin works in people like a plant;
If we want better fruit, we must deal with the chute and the root.*

CHAPTER 1
Study And Application Guide

Warning—DO NOT SKIP

The term "study guide" does **not** mean "you can skip this and go to the next chapter."

Yes, I know this study guide is longer than the entire first chapter, and I am making detailed observations of a long section of text. Please trust me that it is worth your time. If this book is like a foundation for a life with God, then this chapter is the "dirt work" that the foundation must be anchored in. The best foundation would be of little use for building a home if it were floating randomly in a swamp. So please bear with me as I take extra time to make sure we start out "well anchored."

This is boot camp, soldier! Dig in and press on.

Observations Of Romans 1: 18-32

Romans 1:18

> "For the wrath of God is revealed from heaven against all ungodliness and unrighteousness of men who suppress the truth in unrighteousness,"

Notice that when Paul uses the phrase "Wrath of God" here, he does not appear to mean what we typically have in mind when we hear that phrase. In this context there is very little that relates to future "final judgment" or "end times" topics; it's all about the present state of the world. This wrath "is" being revealed—it's happening now. More on this in a few verses.

Paul focuses and elaborates on this phrase in the following verses:

> "Men who suppress the truth."

I'll paraphrase Paul:

> There is one particular characteristic that is common to all of mankind, which is critical to understanding our problem with unrighteousness, ungodliness, and sin (i.e. where all the mess came from). That is, we suppress the Truth of God. We resist it, minimize it, twist it, deny it, corrupt it, abuse it.

Notice the detail and care Paul takes to make sure we don't miss the significance of how people suppress the truth...

Romans 1:19-21

> "...because that which is known about God is evident within them; for God made it evident to them. For since the creation of the world His invisible attributes, His eternal power and divine nature, have been clearly seen, being understood through what has been made, so that they are without excuse. For even though they knew God, they did not honor Him as God or give thanks, but they became futile in their speculations, and their foolish heart was darkened."

God's initial and unchanging purpose for mankind is that we would bear His image—that we would reflect what He is like.[6] With this purpose in mind, God made sure that His True image is clearly seen by everyone and readily available to us all in creation. So, we have no excuse when we reject and deny Him, or more subtly... twist the truth of who He is.

Notice what happens immediately when we fail to "honor" and "thank" God. Our thinking turns to "futile speculations" and our "hearts are darkened." It's the man on the lake! Our perception, desires, and thinking

---

[6] See Genesis 1:26-27 and Appendix 1 for more on the creation of man)

begin to disconnect with what is really true. It's the seed of falsehood taking root in the soil of our soul.

Have you ever seen a "**house of mirrors**" at a carnival? Most of the mirrors twist and distort the original image. That is a great parallel and summary of the history of mankind. We were created to be mirrors that reflect the True image of God. But humans have become more like mirrors that *reject* the image we are supposed to reflect. We suppress and distort it. So now, even though we still have great potential, and even though God has a good eternal purpose in mind for us, people without Christ are not what we were intended to be. It is very difficult to look at most people and see a "good" image of what God is like. Unfortunately, it gets worse as we keep reading.

Romans 1:22-23

> "Professing to be wise, they became fools, and exchanged the glory of the incorruptible God for an image in the form of corruptible man and of birds and for four-footed animals and crawling creatures."

The phrase "exchanged the glory" is used like a synonym for phrase "suppress the truth" from vs 18 above. The phrases are repeated in combination form in verse 25. This helps confirm for us that Paul is continuing his explanation of this same key idea:

> People exchanged the true image of God, which is undeniable in creation, for a corrupted one. Now, that false image is ruining and blinding us.

Mankind's perception of God, and many other important things, is now based on falsehood. All of us are still reflecting "an" image that we have of God deep inside, but it is a distorted image. The seeds of deception are continually being re-planted and re-enforced. As mankind continues along the downward spiral of the corruption of that image, we become more and more convinced of our superior "wisdom," while in reality we are becoming more "foolish." We see this same pattern with the man on the lake. His foolish fear grew tremendously as he became more convinced that the ice could not hold him. Deception reinforces deception.

Romans 1:24-25

> "Therefore God gave them over in the lusts of their hearts to impurity, so that their bodies would be dishonored among them. For they exchanged the truth of God for a lie, and worshiped and served the creature rather than the Creator, who is blessed forever. Amen"

Here we finally see the "wrath of God," which was mentioned in vs 18, in response to mankind's suppression of the truth. This wrath is not nearly so vindictive, or harsh, as many would expect. He simply "gives us over" to the way of thinking we have chosen and the "lust," or evil desire, that results. The wrath described here is not heartless, or an outburst of anger, but it is scary to ponder!

Notice what is present now and also the consequences that are looming on the horizon. All because of the rejection of the Truth and the embrace of falsehood, we now have:

- "Lusts of their hearts" going wild
- "impurity" taking over in their desires
- "bodies dishonored" which indicates sinful action is the next step

It is the dynamics of the plant: root, shoot, fruit!

God really does respect us enough to let us choose what we will think, and as a result what we will feel, want, and do. He lets us have the consequences of our choice of perception, even if that means life without Him.

Romans 1:26-27

> "For this reason God gave them over to degrading passions; for their women exchanged the natural function for that which is unnatural, and in the same way also the men abandoned the natural function of the woman and burned in their desire toward one another, men with men committing indecent acts and receiving in their own persons the due penalty of their error."

It didn't take us long to stumble upon a very controversial topic. I have a few observations of this text that will probably disturb readers on both sides of this issue. I hope we can all be mature enough to set our personal opinions aside for a moment so that we can better understand God's perspective through His Word, written by Paul.

> First, to the conservative, traditional church-going person: please don't try to use this text to alienate or condemn the LGBT community as "worse sinners" than other people. Paul lists homosexuality as <u>one</u> example—one of <u>many</u> examples—in the immediate context, of people's hearts being corrupted by deception from what God originally intended. Be sure to read on to verses 28-32 where several examples of other sins that profoundly separate people from God are found. Many of these other "corruptions" are quite common in conservative churches. I believe this chapter should provoke a sense of humility and compassion for our fellow man within us all—certainly not a holier-than-thou attitude.

Now to the proponents of the LGBT lifestyle: I think the main message to take away from this passage is that "God has something better planned for you." His heart is one of compassion for anyone with "degraded passions" or "burning, unnatural" desires. He knows that is no way to really live. I see Paul sharing and relaying a loving God's frustration with this community for missing out on His better plan. (As a parent who loves my kids, I can relate to God's frustration here!) These words reflect Him longing for something better for them all and distraught over the loss of relationship with so many of His own precious and valuable people over this issue.

Choosing to disagree with Paul and God's Word—to remain "given over" to harmful passions that no one was ever supposed to have—that is certainly an option. Ironically, that is the central theme of this chapter. But it must be acknowledged that Paul lists homosexuality as one of the most obvious examples of corrupted desires and a misled heart. He puts it first in the list, most likely because it is so precisely opposite of what God intended.

Have you begun to notice <u>why people want such evil and impure things?</u> It's not because God's initial design of people is flawed. It's not because it's "just natural"; Paul confirms these desires are most certainly "**unnatural**." What does Romans 1 say is the reason these desires are so often found in the hearts of people? What was the cause for God to give people over to this "indecency"? The phrase "For this reason" ties verses 26 and 27 back to verse 25: "For they exchanged the Truth of God for a lie, and worshipped and served the creature rather than the Creator…"

In other words, we were given over to a degraded, unnatural heart because our perception and worship were set on something besides the true God. I know I sound like a broken record, but so does Paul: it's the Man on ice story and the plant image again. Falsehood and deception are the enemy's "bread and butter"; the kingdom of darkness is based entirely on hiding and twisting the Truth.

What is the "due penalty of their error" from verse 27? Think about the context of the downward spiral of depraved minds and darkened hearts. The due penalty of the error of giving in to homosexuality is… homosexuality itself! It is its own judgment. **The "wrath of God" in response to any sin is… more of that sin** and exposure to more sins, which means less fellowship with Him. Seeds are replanted and false perception is reinforced. It's scary and sobering to me.

Romans 1: 28-32

> "And just as they did not see fit to acknowledge God any longer, God gave them over to a depraved mind, to do those things which are not proper, being filled with all unrighteousness, wickedness, greed, evil; full of envy, murder, strife, deceit, malice; gossips, slanderers, haters of God, insolent, arrogant, boasters, inventors of evil, disobedient to parents, without understanding, untrustworthy, unloving, unmerciful; and although they know the ordinance of God, that those who practice such things are worthy of death, they not only do the same, but also give hearty approval to those who practice them."

Once again, our biggest problem is that we suppress the truth of God. Paul uses a synonymous phrase to re-emphasize his point here: "they did not see fit to acknowledge God."

It is unlikely that you are surprised by the result of this refusal to acknowledge God: "he gave them over." This is the 3rd time in the passage that we have seen the "give people over" description of God's wrath. This time we are given over to a "depraved mind" and then "to do" what is wrong. Notice what we were "filled with" and "full of" (vs 29); these are the things that influenced us to **be** and **do** so much evil. These descriptions are all in line with the same theme we have been reading earlier in the passage; terms like:

- Futile speculations
- Foolish heart darkened
- Became fools
- Hearts lusting for impurity
- Bodies dishonored
- Degrading passions
- Burning unnatural desires

Paul wraps this all up in a nice little "bow of wickedness" by connecting us back to the beginning of the passage with the phrase, "although they know the ordinance of God." We all know better. The truth and ways of God are "evident" to us all (vs 19). We are all "without excuse" (vs 20). But just look at how far down the spiral of depravity we have come. It's a long list of humbling descriptions.

The last crucial phrase that we cannot miss is:

> "They not only do the same, but also **give hearty approval** to those who practice them."

It's one thing when we wrestle with our own issues and when we are our own worst enemy; it's something entirely different when we are encouraging and deliberately influencing others to continue down a path away from God. When we are intentionally spreading the seed of deception to others, we get God's attention in a hurry!

Consider the LGBT controversy as an example from our context. Many on the conservative side point out how homosexuality is often associated with the judgment of God in Scripture. But I don't see much evidence that the real issue is homosexuality being so much worse than other wickedness, or more evil than other evils, more grotesque than greed, more sinister than self-righteousness, or more mortifying than murder. The biggest problem with the LGBT movement, Biblically, is the **intentional influence** it has on other people—particularly young people—to lead them away from God's best. It is the LGBT movement's assertion that the lifestyle is okay, good, and uncorrupt that is the main issue. A movement that promoted greed (mortgage industry fraud), or murder (Nazism), or racism (Nazism again), or religious superiority (Pharisees) would have the same fundamental flaws and meet the same divine opposition that the LGBT movement faces.[7] God certainly wants something better than this for all people, and He will vigilantly protect the innocent from those who threaten to separate them from Him.

---

[7] See Matthew 18:4-6: "but whoever causes one of these little ones who believe in Me to stumble..." Jesus uses strong words here. It would be better not to be one of those "whoevers."

In the same way, "conservative Christian" communities who encourage hatred or violence toward the LGBT community are equally in the wrong. God would certainly oppose a movement of "church" people who attack homosexuals or those struggling with gender identity. God has an agenda; He has very specific motives, which we will explore in some detail later. But for now, we should be clear that He does not "hate sinners." God hates sin, and He loves sinners. Actually, God hates sin **because** He loves sinners. We have seen how sin does such horrible things to those God cares so deeply about. So His passionate opposition of sin makes sense.[8] We would do well to remember that no Christian who confuses "opposition of sin" with "hatred of sinful people" can reflect God's heart very well at all.

Observations Summary Of Romans 1: 18-32

If you were the devil, how would you influence people away from God? Knowing that people are like plants—that the fruit our lives produce is an outgrowth of the seed planted in us—what would your strategy be? Knowing that our lives will reflect the perception of God that we have, how would you try to get us to turn away from God?

The answer is glaringly obvious: **you would lie to people about the heart and motives of God**! You would plant as many seeds of falsehood as possible. If you were the devil you wouldn't be foolish enough to try to get people to go against their good desires; you'd focus your efforts on getting people to want what is bad. It's so simple. And that is exactly what the enemy has done! Root (lies), Shoot (corrupt thoughts and desires), Fruit (evil actions).

---

[8] God does not start with hatred of sin, as some mistakenly teach, and then look for those without sin to decide who to love. God loves the world—He loves us all. Because He loves us all, and sin is so horrible for us, He hates and opposes sin. Yes, His wrath often includes giving us over to sin temporarily. Sometimes, we must take one step backward to realize how desperately we need to take two steps forward.

It doesn't make sense for anyone to trust and honor Someone else when they are suspicious of the other Person's motives. No one would expect the man who was genuinely concerned about the thickness of the ice to feel peaceful walking across it. In the same way, the enemy knows that as long as he manipulates your perception of God, no matter how good God actually is or how wonderful His motives and plans for us really are, we will continue to reject, refuse to honor, and disobey Him. Everyone's life will reflect what we believe deep inside and how we perceive God to be.

Proverbs 27:19 is an excellent concise summary:

"As water reflects the face, so one's life reflects the heart."

All sin on the outside can be traced back to deception on the inside. All fruit grew from a root.

[*Spoiler Alert*: The devil's plan has a critical flaw. Jesus has exploited it in a big way. If the devil's lies are proven beyond a shadow of a doubt to be false, and genuine faith in the Truth of God rises up in us, the entire downward spiral of sin will be profoundly reversed. If you have been stuck or discouraged in your walk with God, stay tuned! You will soon see how the God of hope has focused His almighty power to help you right where you are.]

QUESTIONS FOR REFLECTION AND DISCUSSION

Where did all the mess in the world come from? Why do people, who were created by God in His own good image, desire and do such awful things? How does Paul explain this?

Jeremy Weimer

How do people end up as God-haters? Explain using as many terms from his passage as possible, or give an example that you have seen.

If we were created by God with the intent that we would bear His image, how do so many people end up full of "unrighteousness, wickedness, greed, and evil"? Weren't we created to reflect the God we know? He's not arrogant, boastful, untrustworthy, unloving, or unmerciful, is He? If we are "created in His image" it sounds like He might not be "good" like Christians say He is, or at least that He's not good at creating people who fulfill the purpose He intended. What gives?

Wasn't it because of disobedience that mankind was punished?
Didn't the bad choice come first, and then the fall?
What does Romans chapter 1 say came first?
Maybe we need to look back at the Adam and Eve story a little more closely.
(Stay tuned for Chapter 2 and its study guide)

What examples from your own life, or scripture, help illustrate these dynamics of sin?

Reminder: The biggest question we are ultimately aiming to answer is not "How does sin work?" or "Why is sin so prevalent in the world?" but "How does Christ defeat sin for us?"—both from an eternal and a daily perspective. Paul will cover this in detail in the following chapters of Romans.

CHAPTER 2

WHAT DO I DO NEXT—
NOW THAT I AM A CHRISTIAN?
IT'S NOT UP TO YOU

> "(It) is that which is of the heart, by the Spirit, not by the letter;
> And his 'praise' is not from men but from God."
> —Romans 2:29

So, what do you do now? If you have asked Jesus into your heart, walked out on what you are now realizing is not "thin ice," and trusted Him to save you—if you have asked Him to be your Lord, *what should you do next?* Knowing that the world is under the influence of deception and sin, how can you make a difference and help people?

I love these questions because they show eagerness, hope, and excitement of a life with Christ. But please be careful not to rush the process or get ahead of yourself. Before God can do a work **through** you He needs to do a work **in** you. Before you can be ready for what God ultimately wants *you* to do *in the world*, you first need to go through the process of what **He** wants to do *in you*. I recommend that you reword the question:

"God, now that I am a Christian, what do *you* want to do *in me*?"

Jeremy Weimer

Don't Judge; Don't Hate

Let's pick up where we left off in Romans. After the outright rejection of God that is displayed in the sobering list at the end of Romans 1, what would you expect Paul to address next? Personally, I would have expected a description of how the judgment of God would be coming swiftly upon the "God-haters." We do get a section on judgment in Romans 2, but surprisingly, it is focused more on how God will judge *religious people* who pass judgement those "outright sinners." Be careful about looking down on others!

Circumcision Of The Heart (And Its Source)

Living with *integrity* and the risk of *hypocrisy* for people who judge others and focus too much on doing all the right things on the outside—these are important topics for Paul as he continues in Romans 2. As I mentioned before, many religious people are trying to **get the sin weeds out of their yard** by simply *mowing the grass* instead of letting God deal with the "root" heart and character issues inside. I encourage you to read all of Romans 2, but I want to focus on Paul's conclusion in verses 28 and 29:

> "For he is not a 'Jew' who is one outwardly, nor is 'circumcision' that which is outward in the flesh. But he is a 'Jew' who is one inwardly; and 'circumcision' is that which is of the heart, by the Spirit, not by the letter; and his 'praise' is not from men, but from God."

You will be happy to hear that I do not plan to give a detailed analysis of the Jewish custom of circumcision! I will say that for Paul the term "circumcision" functions as a symbol of living a holy life in the eyes of God. So, what he means here is that living a righteous life by God's own definition is not nearly as much about **what we do** outwardly, but **what He does** inwardly. It's about what He does in our heart by His Spirit, not what we accomplish by our efforts to keep the letter of His law.

Don't miss this shift in strategy; it is subtle, but essential: The way to come to God, and the way to grow closer to God, is not by keeping the letter of the law, not by following religious to-do lists, and not by *pulling ourselves up by our own bootstraps*. Our part is to believe—to believe in what God has done for us and what He is doing in us. The focus shifts from our efforts to His, from our works to His. Only God removes our old, prideful, self-reliant heart; only the Spirit of God makes us new. Our confidence, trust, and hope for a better tomorrow shifts from our own efforts to God and His *circumcision of our heart*.

The Solution Must Address The Real Problem

Reflect back on what Paul explained in Romans 1 about why sin has such a widespread influence on humanity.

- Why does **greed** exist in people?
    - Because we have suppressed the Truth that God rewards and provides faithfully.
    - There would be no desire for *more than we really need* if we were content trusting God to satisfy the good desires He's given us.

- Why are people so quick to **judge** each other and why is **self-righteousness** so prevalent?
    - Because we are created with a moral compass that knows *wrong should be put right*, but we have refused to be patient for God to carry out justice in His time.
    - We wouldn't have the insecurity that drives us to look down on others if we were anchored in the Truth of God's justice (to make things right) and grace (to forgive).

- Why are outbursts of **anger** such common challenges for people?
    - Because as we lost sight of God's sovereign power over our lives, and His good plan to bless us, we get the sense that everything depends on us. And all sorts of little things seem big, as they threaten our sense of control.

> o If we lived with the True perspective that God is in control, and He can use all things for our good, we wouldn't be so easily threatened by circumstances or the poor choices of others.

These are all examples to show that sin exists because of deception in our perception. The point is that greedy, self-righteous, excessively angry people can't solve their own sin problem. Just as an apple tree can't change the type of tree it is by trying to produce bananas, people need help with their heart perspective from beyond themselves. God must intervene to transform us from the inside out—from root to fruit.

Our Identity, Impact, And Legacy

Paul is also using the terms "Jew" and "praise" in a symbolic way to help us understand our true identity and impact. These terms represent:

- Being a child of God in good standing with Him (a "Jew")
- Leaving a legacy of impacting people by honoring God (our "praise")

Here is a paraphrase of Paul's conclusion above:

> A person is not a righteous child of God by being one outwardly, nor does anyone gain right standing with God by some outward religious act. A person is a Christian only by first becoming one inwardly; the essence of good standing with God begins with the heart. Only the Spirit of God removes old hearts and gives new ones—neither the law's written code nor man's efforts to keep it could ever accomplish this. In the deepest sense, no person's identity or impact is determined by human beings—not themselves, nor parents, nor priests. For all of us, "who we really are" is a reflection of our own relationship with God; and that reflection can only be "good" if we have received in our heart the good gift God offers.

It is very dangerous spiritually to assume that our behavior determines our identity or that the eternal impact God wants our lives to have depends too much on us. Our identity and impact depend overwhelmingly on Him! They are in God's hands now. It takes time to see them come to fulfilment, but they are a central part of His gift to you.

CAINE'S IMAGE-FORMING DARK ROOM

Christine Caine, an international speaker from Hillsong Church in Australia, explains this concept brilliantly with the image of an old photo darkroom.[9] She describes how it takes time for the image to be formed on the photo paper and how if light got in the darkroom before the image was fully formed, it would ruin the photo. In the same way, God is forming His True image in us. She summarizes:

> If the world's spotlight that is **on** you is greater than the (gospel's) light that is **in** you, the spotlight will destroy you.

This is true in Hollywood, in professional sports, in politics, and it's true in church. Godly character is the key to your identity and impact, and without it we can't handle the pressures of the spotlight. Your *character* must be established before your *calling* can be fulfilled. God cares about you enough to ask you to be patient so He can give you these inner things—that matter most—first. You are who you are inwardly; and your outer life will reflect that. Give the Spirit of God time to uproot the seeds of deception and establish new roots of True faith so that your life will produce good fruit.[10]

---

[9] Christine Caine Dark Moments of our life
(specifically 6 or 7 minutes from 7:00 to 13:00)
https://www.youtube.com/watch?v=8FLI4F_iz5g
The Gospel Bootcamp website will update links to this video frequently

[10] See chapter 1 for the Root, Shoot, Fruit image.

Reflections On My Own Life

I wish I could tell you that I am a lifelong expert in the area of patience and character so you would have an amazing example to follow. Unfortunately, my life has been more of an example of what happens when Christians don't learn this concept early on. I wish someone had explained this to me over and over again when I was a very young Christian. I almost destroyed my family, and I did ruin many relationships with other Christians. Selfish ambition to climb the ladder of ministry success and "doing great works for God" is deadly. God has been amazingly faithful in spite of my impatience and independence; He has restored so much that I damaged. But that was a grueling road to walk. I pray that you and your family could be spared the anguish.

Conclusion Summary

What do you do next, as a new Christian? Make a solemn resolution not to get too bogged down with outward activities too soon. But that doesn't mean be passive! **Commit to giving yourself wholly to God so He can "develop" you from the inside out.** <u>Give Him permission every day to do whatever He wants within you</u>. When His image is formed in you, then the world will see Him when they watch you. That is what they need; that will be your impact. It's up to Him to see this process through; only He can.

Ask yourself how God feeds and fills you. How do you connect with Him and learn from Him? Prioritize time in those activities.

I *hesitate* to give you a list—seriously, I am very reluctant about spelling out the activities below because it can be so easy to get lost in the activities and forget that they are useless if God is not working in us through the activity.

Please remember: you are not *required* to do *any* of these. Choose the ones you *want* to do. God is developing a new heart in you with new desires: delight in Him through these activities—indulge!

Here are some ways that believers through history have made room for God to work in their lives and prioritized relationship with Him in their hearts:

- Read the Scriptures
- Pray or journal prayers
- Be part of a church small group within a local church community
- Serve someone—meet a practical need without expecting repayment from them
- Find a mentor who can help guide you in the journey with God
- Invest in someone who is younger in the faith than you
- Read a Christian book
  (you can check this off "the list," but only if you read the study guides too ☺)

Just like a photograph in an old photo darkroom,
The image must be developed over time before we are ready for display.

Chapter 2
Study and Application Guide

Read the Appendix

The appendix is the study guide for this chapter. Don't miss out!

> Yes, I know that only about 11% of the population reads the appendix of books.
>
> Read this one.
>
> Yes, I am aware that the common understanding of the word "appendix" is:
>
>> "the chapter at the end that you don't need to read." ☺
>
> You need to read this one!
>
> Yes, I know that half of my readers have never read an appendix in their life.
>
> This is boot camp; we're going to try some new things!

Without the background of Genesis 1-3, it will be very difficult to follow Paul through Romans or to appreciate the beauty and power of what Christ has done for us on the Cross.

CHAPTER 3

How Does The Process Work?
Salvation By Revelation

> "...the redemption which is in Christ Jesus...
> was **to demonstrate His righteousness**..."
> – Romans 3:24-25

Unhelpful Explanations When We Need Practical Solutions

How does what Christ did 2,000 years ago actually make a practical difference in our everyday lives now? Why does a price paid so long ago still matter so much today?

As you live this new life with God, if you are "all-in" with your commitment to the process of being transformed into His image, you will face some "dark rooms." You will face hard times, disappointment, loss, temptation, pain, offense. You will definitely need help being a different person and responding differently than you have in the past. Would you like to know how the power of the gospel and the message of the cross works to help you in these critical situations?

Let's start with how this topic is most commonly explained.[11] Usually, when I talk to people about what difference the cross makes, they say something like: "Because Jesus died in my place, I'm forgiven." That is absolutely true; the Bible does say that, but how does it work? If a

---
[11] Please bear with me as I play *devil's advocate* to help illustrate this point.

murderer is convicted and sentenced to the death penalty, but someone else chooses to die in his place, the murderer is still guilty. Plus, he is still the same person with the same tendencies that led him to the offense in the first place. Has anything changed? This kind of "legal pardon" forgiveness seems more like injustice, and denial of reality, than anything desirable. Most of us need more help than this explanation offers.

I also often hear the explanation: "Jesus paid the price for my sins, so I don't need to." This is also true; we won't be required to pay the penalty that the law demands for our sins. But who is demanding that price be paid? Is it God, to satisfy His wrath? That would not paint a picture of grace or love; it sounds more legalistic, full of vengeance, even bloodthirsty.[12] Is it the devil? Did the devil need to be "paid off" to satisfy the penalty for our sins? This is getting messy, but I do think it's helpful to ask:

> Who is demanding that the price be paid?

THE TRUE PURPOSE OF THE CROSS ACCORDING TO PAUL

Paul explains the purpose and mechanics of Christ's sacrifice in careful detail, but I'll warn you: Paul would have failed 6th grade English because of his love of run-on sentences![13] Take your time reading through Romans 3:21-26, and I'll help simplify below:

> "But now... the **righteousness of God has been manifested**... through faith in Jesus Christ for all those who believe... for all have sinned and fall short of the glory of God, being justified as a gift by his grace through the redemption which is in Christ

---

[12] Remember that the Mosaic law was added later (Galatians 3:17, 19) to help make us aware of the seriousness of our sin (Romans 3:20). The establishment of the law by God, unyielding as the law itself may be, was actually done in mercy—as part of His loving plan of redemption. More on this in a later chapter, but know for now that the Mosaic law was not eternal; it was in effect temporarily to set up the eternal message of the gospel of Christ.

[13] For Paul, everything connected. All the concepts, images, and stories in the Bible fit together into one unified message for him. So, I am convinced that part of his goal in writing these "epic" sentences was to help us connect the concepts in our own minds.

Jesus; whom God displayed publically as a propitiation in His blood through faith... **to demonstrate His righteousness**, because in the forbearance of God He passed over the sins previously committed—**for the demonstration of His righteousness** at the present time, so that He would be just and the justifier of the one who has faith in Jesus."

Can we please have a new subject and verb? There must have been a famine of periods in Paul's day.

One simple Bible study technique that helps us digest long complex passages is to *notice what is repeated*. This is almost always where the author's emphasis will be. Twice in the passage above Paul says the purpose of all this was to "demonstrate (God's) righteousness." The main subject and verb of the whole monstrous sentence is also that the "righteousness of God has been manifested" or revealed, which is basically a synonym for "demonstrated." So that adds clarity and emphasis to Paul's simple point here:

> This is what the cross is all about: demonstrating God's righteousness, revealing His goodness and character, proving the loving intent of His heart toward us.

How This Demonstration Helps

The gospel's demonstration is powerful because it is the perfect solution to humanity's central problem. Paul described our issue so carefully in Romans 1 – 3 because he wants us to be able to fully appreciate the resolution God has provided. Throughout the Bible we see a clear message of mankind's struggle with the Truth of God, which makes it challenging to trust Him:

> Deep in the heart of people worldwide the motives of God are on trial and His Truth is under scrutiny.

This is part of the fallout from the seeds of doubt that the enemy planted in the garden of Eden. I will confess that my heart is often like a courtroom. Especially when I face hardship, disappointment, loss—I know God is powerful enough to change circumstances that I don't like. Why doesn't He?

Paul explains that the gospel helps us with the trial in our heart. God is the one being accused. Jesus' sacrifice of Himself is the hard evidence that God's motives can absolutely be trusted. There is no other plausible explanation to motivate Jesus to go through with the crucifixion than that deep down, God's heart is to put us before Himself. His eternal desire and decision is to put our good before His own comfort. That is genuine love.[14] If there was ever a time when God would have failed us—if there was ever a situation when He would have decided that the cost was too high and we were not worth the price to save us, it would have been at the cross. The good news of the gospel is:

> The cross is the **absolute proof** that God's righteousness is for real, His character is without blemish, His heart is completely without the corruption of selfishness.

This is the best news in all of history! The ice is rock solid. You can trust God wholeheartedly—we have proof! It's the same principle of proof that the man on the lake experienced, but on a much larger level. The horses pulling the sled may have completely transformed the scared man's day by proving the strength of the ice; but Jesus' sacrifice on the cross will transform our eternity by proving the good heart of God!

REAL FORGIVENESS AND THE PRICE DEMANDED FOR IT

Paul's insight here into how the gospel practically works in our lives has more implications than I could possibly fit into one chapter. But let's

---

[14] Greater love has no man than this, that he would lay down his life for his friends. John 15:13

consider two that I mentioned above: **forgiveness** and *who* **needed the price to be paid**.

The forgiveness that the gospel's revelation gives us is a genuine and life-changing transformation, not a surface and petty pardon:

> In the same way that the devil used **deception** to corrupt our perception and *make us sinners*, God uses **revelation** to correct our perception and *re-make us as righteous*.

Through the cross God destroys the works of the devil.[15] By whispering "the ice is not trustworthy—probably paper thin," the devil had us cowering in fear. But Jesus demonstrates with perfect certainty that stepping out with bold faith in God is walking on solid ground. We may as well drive a tank out on His frozen lake because He is only good and infinitely strong! This is true forgiveness. God does not simply excuse our faith failures from the past; He empowers us with evidence to support our faith for the future.

He is "**just** and the **justifier** of the one who has faith in Jesus" from verse 26 above. These are the same Greek words that are usually translated "righteous." So Paul is saying:

> By meeting the righteous requirements of the law in our place, God is not only demonstrating His own righteousness to us, but in doing that He is also **making us righteous**.

We are not simply given a label of being "righteous" that only has meaning in some distant mystical "positional" reality. God's *demonstration* genuinely purges our hearts of *deception*. In other words, revelation is the basis of true salvation. The proof God gives provides us power to live—and actually **be** righteous.

---

[15] 1 John 3:8— ...The Son of God appeared for this purpose: to destroy the works of the devil.

This leads us to the "**who** demanded the price" question. God didn't need to vent His wrath on Jesus in some kind of cosmic temper-tantrum to "get over" Himself. **We** needed the price to be paid. In our fallen skepticism, you and I demanded proof that the character of God is reliable. We needed evidence of God's love and care for us—evidence that would stand up in the "courtroom" of our own hearts. God had no obligation to prove Himself, but He cared enough to give us the proof we desperately needed instead of the judgement that we deserved. We are genuinely forgiven now, not because Christ's sacrifice allows God to go into some type of *denial* about what we have done or who we are. Christ's offering on the cross actually changes who we are! The old tree of sin is cut off at the root, and a new life of faith begins—a life that is grounded in a True knowledge of the good heart of God.[16]

Does It Really Work?

This gospel of the revelation of the goodness of God—does it actually work in a powerful, life-changing way? (Be sure to continue on to chapter 4 for several examples.) For now, I can speak confidently that my own life has been profoundly changed through the process Paul explains here in Romans. I've asked God to help me share one example from my own life to encourage you:

> Before I encountered God through the message of the cross, I had an anger problem with Him. I was already trying to serve Him, but when things didn't go my way I would get furious—at Him! I thought I was trusting Him with my life, but I felt abandoned—kicked to the curb—when times got hard. But over time, I experienced more and more of God's patience and kindness with me. He proved that He loved me once-and-for-all at the cross.
>
> The good seeds of faith that were planted in me began to grow in my soul. Eventually, I came to the point where I became convinced

---

[16] More on this transformation in chapter 6 and 7.

that He had my best interests in mind no matter what happened. Now, even when circumstances are very hard, I end up thankful. I may still get frustrated; I may wish for something else initially. But then He reminds me that He's using the challenges for my good and the good of those I love. I don't need to be in control, or get my way, or even understand how all the details will work out. I know Him, His heart, and the loving intent of all of His motives. So, I have peace and thankfulness that is stable in hard times. This is the divine power of God working in me... through the cross... by revealing His goodness, character, righteousness, His pure love.

IT WILL WORK FOR YOU TOO

Spend some time in prayer, and ask God to show **you** His heart through the story of the cross. Ask Him to demonstrate His character, His faithfulness, His trustworthiness, kindness, compassion, and determination to have a friendship with you—right in the middle of the challenges in your life. If nothing else, be honest with Him if you have a "courtroom" situation going on in your own heart. If you're having trouble trusting Him because of certain situation, talk to Him bluntly about it. He won't be surprised! Avoiding the issue won't help.

Be willing to believe what His Word says is true, despite how you feel or how things seem. You may find that you need to step out on what "appears" to be *thin ice* before you get the revelation that the ice is more reliable than you ever imagined. Then, be patient with yourself. It may take a little time for it to "click" inside of you, but this **is** how the cross works.

*God's motives and faithfulness are on trial within each of us;
Jesus' sacrifice is the "hard evidence" proof that helps us with our verdict.*

CHAPTER 3
STUDY AND APPLICATION GUIDE

Reflect back to Paul's thesis from Romans 1:16-17 for confirmation of the main point he is making:

> "…I am not ashamed of the gospel, for it is the power of God for salvation to everyone who believes… for in it the righteousness of God is revealed, from faith to faith; as it is written, 'but the righteous will live by faith.'"

- Why is the power of God for salvation inseparable from the gospel?
    - Because only in the gospel is the righteousness of God so profoundly revealed/demonstrated
    - From ch. 1, Satan's power to corrupt hearts depends on the propagation of Lies
    - From ch. 3, God's power to cleanse hearts depends on the revelation of Truth
- How would you explain the way the gospel helps you in your life?

In 3:24 Paul writes that we are "justified through the redemption"; this speaks of people being made righteous through a price that was paid.

Also, in 3:25, Paul writes that "God displayed Jesus as a propitiation"; this refers to a sacrificial ceremony where an offering was made to satisfy demands of a religious code.

- How does the price Jesus paid make a difference for you in the day-to-day?

- How does His sacrifice to meet the requirements of the law help you trust His heart? (Try to give an answer that is both personal and practical).

Here are a few verses from the gospels about Christ, the pinnacle of His life being his sacrifice on the cross, and the purpose behind that offering. What do these reveal about the heart of God toward you?

Matthew 20:28 / Mark 10:45

> "...the Son of Man did not come to be served, but to serve, and to give his life as a ransom for many."

John 1: 17-18 (paraphrase)

> "For the law was given through Moses; grace and truth came through Jesus Christ. No one has ever seen God, the one and only Son, who is himself God and in the intimate embrace of the Father, He has made Him known."

John 8: 32

> (Jesus speaking) "...you will know the Truth, and the Truth will set you free."

John 14: 6, 9

> (Jesus speaking) "I am... the Truth... He who has seen Me has seen the Father."

John 16: 25, 27, 29-30 (paraphrase)

> (Jesus speaking) "… an hour is coming when I will no longer speak to you in figurative language… for the Father Himself loves you…"
>
> (the disciples reply) "Oh! Now you're speaking plainly… Now we get it!"

Again, what does Jesus' "ultimate act of service" in dying for us on the cross reveal about Him and the intentions of God toward you and me?

CHAPTER 4

What Does God See?
Examples of the Gospel's Process Working: What God concludes when He sees Faith

> "…Abraham believed God, and it was 'credited'
> to him as righteousness…"
> –Romans 4:3

Heroes With Some "History," Patriarchs With A "Past"

<u>David</u>: Have you ever wondered how God could look at David, a murderer and adulterer, and conclude:

> "He is a man after My own heart. I think I'll have him write the ultimate book on worshipping Me, the Psalms"?

<u>Paul</u>: Here's another "exemplary" hero of the faith. He was the ring-leader who orchestrated a mob execution of the first Christian martyr. He was also one of the most strictly religious keepers of the Jewish law—one who despised non-Jews. God looked at him and said:

> "Oh, this is the perfect missionary apostle to the Gentiles. I'll have him write most of the New Testament and be the one to explain the gospel of grace apart from the law—how Jesus died for everyone— to the Non-Jewish world."

Peter: He was impulsive, a blabbermouth, and cowardly. He denied Christ three times in His hour of greatest need. He was even intimidated by a servant girl. But God saw that there was much more potential in Peter. God saw a rock. He saw the man who would be a key leader of the early church. God says of him:

> "This one! This is the perfect person for me to count on to stand up in front of the Jewish community that just crucified My Son and tell them: 'You fools just killed the Messiah! And you're in a heap of trouble if you don't get right with Him (Acts 2 paraphrase).'"

Peter had the perfect qualifications, right?

Gideon: He was cowardly—hiding from the enemies of God's people. God addressed him as "mighty man of valor." He wasn't mocking him; God saw the warrior inside. Gideon eventually led God's people to freedom through victory in a battle where he was insanely outnumbered—most likely outmanned more than 100 to 1. How did God know where cowardly Gideon would end up?

Moses: He had anger-management issues and a speech impediment. God saw the perfect guy to be the representative speaker before the most powerful ruler in the world of his day. He was the ideal candidate to explain to Pharaoh that he must let the nation's entire work force just walk away. Makes perfect sense, right?

Solomon: 700 wives and 300 concubines. Can you imagine the absurd mess that he got himself into in his home? God says:

> "Here's my guy! This is the one who will write the book on wisdom for simplifying your life and avoiding foolishness (Proverbs). I think I'll have him write the book on romance and passionate devotion to your spouse in marriage too." (Song of Solomon)

I don't know about you, but if I owned a big company, I would not hire God as the recruiting manager. He seems to be oblivious to resumes and character assessment!

The entire Bible is full of stories of people being corrupted by the enemy's deception, but then many of them end up profoundly transformed after encountering God. How did He know that these people with such catastrophic failures in their past had such incredible potential for the future? How does He do His evaluation process? How could He tell that their temporary character flaws would not define their eternal destiny? It's actually surprisingly simple:

> God does not define any of us by our past actions or our current soul condition; He looks at the heart.[17] He knows that if there is a true faith perspective of Himself deep within us, then everything else will be transformed from the inside out.

God knows that the old plant and old fruit that may have grown from seeds of deception are not nearly as important in determining our future destiny as the current Truth we are believing about Him now. He is not depending on people to transform themselves when He sees us in the "dark room"; His Spirit within us will establish the image He wants to see. Regardless of where we are, or who we may have been in the past, when God notices that our hearts now "see Him as He truly is," He knows we are already changed. He looks ahead to what the future will be for us; He can see the fruit that faith will produce. This is a huge reason why there is tremendous hope for you and me!

---

[17] 1 Samuel 16 – "God sees not as man sees, for man looks at the outward appearance, but the LorD looks at the heart."

Jeremy Weimer

God The Father's Assessment Of "The" Father Of Faith

Paul references <u>Abraham</u>'s story in Romans 4, as he explains the relationship between our faith, our works, and God's work through the gospel to transform us:

> "…Abraham believed God, and it was 'credited' to him as righteousness…" (verse 3)

Here's another shameless plug for reading the Bible in context:

> Whenever another Scripture passage is quoted, it's critical to look up that passage in its own original context.

The quote Paul uses comes from Genesis 15. Take a few minutes to read that chapter too. God appears to Abraham with a promise of great encouragement. But Abraham's faith is still growing. The man who would become a hero of the faith—even the father of faith[18]—is here whining about his circumstances, wondering how things will work out, and very impatient as he waits for God.[19]

In the same way that the gospel helps us believe today, in Genesis 15 God helped Abraham believe by revealing Himself and His plan for Abraham through a promise. It was when Abraham realized that God had planned (and was determined) to bless him, despite his circumstances, that his whole perspective changed. It finally clicked within Abraham that the outcome he desired depended much more on God than anything else—including himself or his wife. Because of faith, Abraham became a new man, and God confirmed it by concluding that he was now righteous.

---

[18] Romans 4:16-17 – we are all of the faith of Abraham; he is the father of us all… a father of many nations

[19] Don't be discouraged if you have "what can You give me to make up for this mess" moments with God like Abraham does here. "How can this possibly work out?" is a normal question that every genuine believer will ask at times. Feeling that way is probably a great indication that you have trusted God enough to allow Him to bring you to a "dark room." You may be on the threshold of a faith breakthrough!

The Greek word translated "credited" or "reckon" in Romans 4:3 is critically important to the message of Paul's chapter. It appears only 40 times in the entire Bible, but an amazing 11 times in Romans 4. No other book of the Bible has more than 7 occurrences of the word. Logizomai sounds like "log-itz-o-my," and reminds me of making a "log" to keep track of something. It literally means to take account of something and come to a conclusion about it—to analyze and based on the analysis to think a certain way. So what we have in Romans 4 is a clear explanation of how God thinks about us—how He takes account of us and comes to His conclusion about us.

This paraphrase of Romans 4:3, with the meaning of logizomai spelled out, can help us grasp Paul's point:

> ...Abraham believed God, and God noticed; God was carefully assessing his heart. When He saw True faith He concluded that Abraham was righteous.

Here is the principle that Paul is helping us understand about how God measures us:

When He takes inventory of our heart and sees true faith, He concludes we are righteous.

This conclusion is perfectly consistent with how Paul initially described God's assessment of us in Romans 1. When God saw lack of faith (or corrupted perspective) in us, He knew the future fruit would be a disaster for our souls. He knew the unrighteousness that would result from the seeds of deception that were planted. So, He allowed the process of "mind depravity" and "heart darkening" to take place. This was in hope that that our sin would be exposed and we would eventually turn back to Him.

Now here in Romans 4 we still have God operating in the same principle: He still sees the end from the beginning, but Abraham is moving in the opposite direction. God sees genuine faith in Abraham (and in us). He knows the fruit of a righteous life that will result. So, as he sees Abraham's faith (and ours), God concludes that Abraham is righteous (and so are we). God is not at all mistaken in His assessment. The rest of Abraham's life, and his legacy through history, confirm that God was correct in His "righteous" conclusion; our life and legacy will prove Him right as well.

CERTAIN HELP IN UNCERTAIN SITUATIONS

The second half of Genesis 15 encourages me greatly. Even after Abraham believed, and after God concluded that he was righteous, Abraham still wrestled to believe what seemed impossible. In Genesis 15:8, he asks, "Oh Lord God, how may I <u>know</u> that I will possess it?" I can relate. That courtroom scene still arises in my heart where God's trustworthiness is in question in the face of incredible "dark room" odds and what sometimes seems to be "thin ice." It is true that Romans 4:18-21 describes Abraham *eventually* living with:

- "against all hope" faith
- "unwavering" faith
- supernatural "power over death" faith

But *he did not get there in an instant.* There was a growth process that Abraham stumbled through like the rest of us.

Notice how God helped strengthen Abraham's developing faith in Genesis 15. In exactly the same way that Christ's sacrifice proves the loving heart and unwavering character of God for us, the Lord also provided a sacrifice for Abraham in his day. God provided proof with the most solemn covenant promise that could be made in that day's culture, and He told Abraham, "Know for certain…" (v 13). That is the kind of help I need. This is what Paul is explaining through the first several chapters of Romans: we can all *know for certain,* because of the incredible price Christ paid, how perfectly good and faithful God is to us.

Faith And Forgiveness: The Spirit's "Clean Slate"

I will conclude this chapter with another important reference that Paul gives in Romans 4:6-8. But I will also include the next verse from the Old Testament passage (since I'm a compulsive context junkie!):

> "Blessed are those whose lawless deeds have been <u>forgiven</u>,
> And whose sins have been covered.
> Blessed is the man whose sin the LORD will not take into account,
> And <u>in whose spirit there is no deceit</u>."
>
> Romans 4 and Psalm 32

Notice the essential connection here between forgiveness and truth deep within us. God's forgiveness of all the heroes of the faith (and us), is not a "token" or look-the-other-way forgiveness. The forgiveness God offers a legitimate release from sin and sinfulness in our core. The deceit within us that originally made us unrighteous is gone. True faith resides within us now, and "righteous" is the correct assessment.

Conclusions—Both God's And Your Own

My challenge to you in this chapter is to **let what is most important to God be what is most important to you**. Don't focus on past performance or religious "works" when you evaluate[20] yourself and others. Ask God for insight into the faith perspective of the heart; that is where His attention is anyway. Our deep inner perspective, whether based on truth or deception, will influence the fruit of our lives more than any other outward factor.

David, Paul, Peter, Gideon, Moses, Solomon—they all went through this same basic perspective-purging process, much like Abraham. God saw

---

[20] See note above on "credited" / logizomai. "Evaluate" is another great synonym for this word.

much more in these men than what their past and present would indicate. We should not be surprised that God was absolutely correct!

When God looks at you, what does He see? What does He conclude? If you have lied in the past, He may not see a liar. If you have made cowardly decisions, He may not see a coward. If you have blown up in anger or violence, He might already see how kind you will be.

The essential first question is: **how do you see Him?** If you still have a big problem with your perception of God, Jesus can help you with that! If He can transform Paul, Peter, Gideon, Moses, Solomon, David, and Abraham by faith, He is not at all intimidated by you or the help you may need to believe.

Also of great importance is: **how do you see yourself?** If God looks deep within you and gives you "righteousness credit" based on your faith in Him… who are you to argue with Him? In other words, if God sees that you are righteous, should you still consider yourself to be a sinner?

God has taken a careful look at our hearts and made His assessment; What did He conclude about you?

CHAPTER 4
STUDY AND APPLICATION GUIDE

What on earth was God thinking when He chose these "severely disqualified" Bible heroes and described them the way He did?

What does God see when He looks at us? What does He conclude about us when He sees True faith deep within us?

>   (Psalm 139 could be a helpful reference)

What is the meaning of the phrase God "credits us with righteousness," as He did with Abraham? Describe what Paul means by this phrase in your own words?

How do you explain the way Abraham still had some doubts and struggles with uncertainty even after he was confirmed as "righteous" by God because of his faith?

>   (Don't worry if you find this hard to explain. Paul isn't finished with this topic—not until at least chapter 7!)

Jeremy Weimer

What does forgiveness have to do with faith and deceit?

In a church full of genuine believers, do you think this is an appropriate statement?

> "We're all sinners saved by grace."

CHAPTER 5

WHAT SHOULD I EXPECT NEXT?
THE "IMPOSSIBLE" PART IS ALREADY DONE

If "while we were still sinners… much more then…"
–Romans 5: 8-10

QUICK SUMMARY

> Ch. 1: We know where all the mess in the world came from: deception about God is the root of sin.
>
> Ch. 2: We know that God is the One freeing us from influence of sin and deception, through the "dark room" process that takes some time.
>
> Ch.3: We know *how* He frees us: through revelation of His Truth by demonstrating His loving heart.
>
> Ch.4: We know that once God sees the seed of True faith planted in us, He already considers us righteous, even if the change is not evident on the outside yet.

Based on all this, how should our expectations for the future change?

Transformation of Expectations

We tend to expect that how things have been is how they will be. Examples:

> Gravity: if I drop something heavy, I expect it will fall.
> Oxygen: if I run as fast as I can, I expect to get winded.

I've observed and experienced these things in the past, so I know what to expect in the future.

The devil knows that people function this way, and he uses this to his advantage. In fact, one of the enemy's most powerful lies is "things will always be this way":

- You have always been a workaholic. It's just who you are.
- Anxiety has always gotten the best of you. Accept it.
- You are an alcoholic/addict. Nothing can change that.
- You'll never get out of debt. If you could have, you would have by now.
- You'll never have friends. You've always been an outcast.

Does any of this sound familiar?

In Romans 5, Paul explains that because of the life-altering impact of the gospel on us, *we should expect something completely different* than what we have experienced in the past:

> "But God demonstrates His own love for us in that while we were still sinners, Christ died for us. Much more then, now that we have been justified by His blood, we will be saved from the wrath of God through him. For if while we were enemies (of Him) we were reconciled to God through the death of His Son, much more, now that we have been reconciled, we will be saved by His life."

Notice that Paul's explanation here rests on the fact that we have been changed; we are no longer "still sinners," but instead "justified," which is the exact same Greek word translated "righteous" elsewhere in Romans. Part of the reason that God's righteousness is so powerfully revealed to us in the gospel is because it is the story of how He loved us when we were so unlovable—while we were sinners deep within. Now that we have been touched by His love, seen Him as He really is, and believed the Truth, we have been made righteous "by His blood" through faith, just like Abraham. We are not who we once were any longer.

Notice also that the term "wrath" in this context has two important aspects (it's a little different than in Chapter 1):

- "Day of judgment/eternal" wrath[21]
- "Here-and-now/daily downward spiral into sinfulness" wrath[22] (which we have covered in ch 1).

Paul is saying that the gospel unleashes the power of God in our lives to save us from **both** aspects of His wrath. We should be careful not to assume that only "salvation for eternity" is God's gift, while day-to-day progress toward outward transformation is up to us. Paul says the power of God is working through the gospel in both areas. In other words, you should expect to be accepted by God on the day of judgment because of the faith He has planted within you—AND, despite all you may have experienced in your life to this point, because of that same faith, you should also expect to grow in outward habits of godly character. The good news is that because of the gospel you should expect to become more like Jesus on the outside too.

How things have always been does not necessarily keep us bound; our past failures can actually become part of what God uses to set us free. The life-changing power of the cross leverages off the sad reality of who we were when God chose to prove His love for us in this extravagant way. In

---

[21] See Romans 2:5, 8
[22] See Romans 1:18 through the end of the chapter and 4:15

the gospel, *God uses the contrast* of our sinfulness to profoundly illustrate His goodness. What kind of unfathomable love must He actually have for us to die for us in the way He did, *especially when we were so deceived and hostile toward Him?* The gospel works like a catapult: the further we are first pulled by sin away from God the more power will be available to propel us toward God when His Truth finally "clicks" within us. "He who has been forgiven much loves much."[23]

Bird's Eye View Of The Central Message Of Romans

I find it helpful to frequently reference Paul's thesis statement for the entire letter to the Romans:

> "For I am not ashamed of the gospel for it is the power of God for salvation to those who believe—to the Jew first and also to the Greek; for in (the gospel) the righteousness of God is revealed, from faith to (ever increasing) faith. As it is written, 'But the righteous will live by faith.'" (1:16-17)

Everything Paul writes in the Romans is unpacking this statement; it is quite simple, yet eternally profound. Why is the power of God to save people from sin inseparable from the gospel message? It is because through the gospel the righteous character of God is revealed—demonstrated beyond question. It is deception about God that trapped us in sin (Romans 1); only the message of Truth has the power to set us free (Romans 3 and 5).

Since God was willing to endure the excruciating agony of the cross to transform us from being sinners to being righteous, shouldn't we expect Him to finish His work and help us act like the new people we already are? The "impossible" part is done; He already changed us in the deepest part of who we are. "How much more" is He able to help us act like it!

---

[23] Luke 7- Jesus tells a great story that illustrates the same point Paul is making in Romans 5.

"Depends On Me" Disease

I have a disease called "I-Think-It-All-Depends-On-Me" (IDIOT). (Those are not the first letters of the words, but "Idiot" is much easier to remember.) This is an exhausting and debilitating condition because it feeds stress and anxiety. As I try to change my life from sinful to godly, I am like an ant, trying to move a huge ant hill from one place to another. God can scoop up the entire hill and move it with one shovel-full in an instant. But "Idiot" disease keeps me focused on what I can do. So the task seems overwhelming. It causes hope for the future to appear very dim.

But there is another factor at work in me. I have met the "Big Man with the shovel." I'm getting to know Him, and He's a good guy. He made me a promise: that He would move this mountain-like ant hill for me. That promise settled in my Idiot-infected heart. The ant-hill still looks huge to me. I still get overwhelmed sometimes when I think about moving it myself. But then I remember the Big Man; He is more than able to handle this, and He keeps His promises. So I confidently expect that He will get that ant hill moved. Now my symptoms are easing. This doesn't all depend on me, but instead on Him.

"Hope Check" Conclusion

Think about your own expectations. Where do you think your life will end up? What is in store for your family, your career, your relationships? Most importantly: *how does God figure into what you are expecting?* Is the power of the gospel a major factor in your assessment?

Have God's promises and the work He has done in you impacted your outlook on life? Or are you plagued with some of the symptoms of Idiot-disease too? Could your expectations be based too heavily on past experience, what you can do, your education, your bank account, your job, the current state of your relationships—instead of the most important factor of all, the One with the heart and power to change them all?

God is the biggest factor with the most influence on the final outcome of our lives. Spend some time in prayer about this. Ask a friend in the faith for some honest feedback on the kind of expectations that you appear to live with. Let's be sure the "ant's" strength and the "ant's" perspective of the size of the mountain are not the basis for our hope and confidence. The impossible part is done; now we are just waiting on the fruit to grow. Do you expect that a harvest of godly fruit is looming on the horizon of your life?

We have a saying at my church that we repeat every week:

> The best is yet to come!

This isn't just wishful thinking. It's a deep confidence and well-grounded anticipation that we have because of the gospel. If you don't have the same hopeful expectation, ask God to help you grow in this area. He's eager for the invitation!

I pray that this paraphrase of Romans 5:1-10 is a powerful encouragement to you:

> Since we have been made righteous by a new root of faith in the core of our being, we erupt with joy. That joy comes from our genuine expectation that we will one day reflect the righteous glory of God on the outside too. From this new perspective, even trials and tribulations feed our joy. Why joy in trials? Because we know those help transform us to be more like God in character.
>
> Our history and habits don't lead us to disappointment either. Instead, the Holy Spirit helps us appreciate the incredible love of God even more profoundly in view of our sin and past. If His love through the cross is powerful enough to change us from sinners to righteous—from God's enemies to His friends—it is certainly able to help us act like it!

We have every reason to expect "mountains to move" spiritually;
Who do your "great expectations" depend on?

CHAPTER 5
Study And Application Guide

What is an area in your life where you have "things will always be this way" thinking habits but where God, through the gospel, says you should expect something different?

Paul is careful to explain in Romans 5:8-10 that salvation and "being saved" by God has two parts:

- The **Eternal** salvation from being a sinner to a righteous person in the core of who we are

- The **Day-by-day** salvation from sinful habits and the ongoing influence of deception

We need God's help with both; but which one does Paul say is more amazing—almost unfathomable? And which one should we certainly expect God to help us with, in view of the other?

What keeps you from living with that certain expectation, or what Paul calls "much more then" faith?

What symptoms of "I Think It All Depends On Me" disease are most common for you?

CHAPTER 6
What Are We Supposed To Do?
The First Command in Romans

"Consider yourselves to be dead to sin, but alive to God."
–Romans 6:11

Paul's Crescendo To A Command

If you are experiencing a sense of "information overload," you are not alone. Paul is not giving us "bits and pieces" to wrestle with a little at a time. He is unpacking the whole gospel in one letter. He didn't have the luxury of smartphone messaging to allow back-and-forth communication within a few seconds. The trip to get a letter one way to Rome most likely took weeks. Romans is the unabridged version.

Let's recap the practical commands that Paul has given us so far in the first five chapters: Well… there are none. I find this hard to believe, but I don't see a single command in the first five-and-a-half chapters—not one "go and do…" not the first "thou shalt…" Romans 1 – 6:10 is all information to shape our outlook and perspective. This is significant because it means Paul has been working extremely hard to get to this one simple practical conclusion:

The most important factor that changes who we are on the <u>inside</u> is:

"What do we believe <u>about God</u>?" (Chapters 1 – 5)

> But the critical practical choice that causes the inner change to impact our <u>outside</u> habits in the world is:
>
> "What do we believe <u>about ourselves</u>?" (Chapters 6 – 7)

Here is the first command in the book of Romans:

> "…<u>Consider yourselves to be dead to sin, but alive to God</u> in Christ Jesus. Therefore do not let sin reign in your mortal body so that you obey its evil desires… present yourselves to God <u>as those alive from the dead</u>" (6:11-13).

Think of yourself differently. That is practical step 1. We are now dead to sin and alive to God because of the True faith God has planted in us. Your body and flesh may still crave sinful things and oppose the ways of God, but the new *real* you, deeper inside, wants God Himself more than anything else. You are now inclined to everything God wants for you.

Give Yourself Some "Consideration"

You will probably recognize the Greek word that is translated "consider" here; it is a familiar one, although it was translated differently in chapter 4: Logizomai. It's often translated: consider, think of, reckon, account, credit. Back in chapter 4 we learned that God thinks of you differently now. God saw the faith in Abraham's heart and concluded he was righteous (Romans 4:3). God has also taken inventory of your inner man and concluded that you are inclined to *righteousness* (and destined for it) because of the faith alive in you. Now it is time for you to make a bold decision to think of yourself that same way too.

It is now your nature to seek God and do the will of God; you are eternally alive to Him and His ways. That is His gift to you—the result of the faith He paid for you to have. You may be thinking:

> "That's impossible! I have faith in God and a relationship with Jesus, but I also still have many of the corrupt desires and inclinations that were a part of my life before I met Jesus. You're crazy to say that my 'nature' is to do the will of God."

I wrestle with the same conflict—believe me! For now, I want to be clear about what the Word of God says. Peter also makes the same claim as a foundational starting point for the Christian life:

> "…God's divine power has granted us everything pertaining to life and godliness through the True knowledge of Him who called us by His own glory and excellence, for by these He has granted to us His most precious and magnificent promises: that by them <u>you may become **partakers of the divine nature**, having escaped the corruption that is in the world through (evil desires)</u>. (2 Peter 1:3-4)

It is finished. The impossible part is done. God has re-made us to share in His own righteous nature[24] and free us from the corruption of sin. The question is: will we believe it? We need to *exercise faith in God's work within us **before** we will see much outward evidence of that inward miracle.*

If this "divine nature" concept of yourself makes you uncomfortable and turns your theology upside down, don't blame me. I would have never come up with something that radical on my own! You will need to file your complaint with the Lord and take up the issue with Paul and Peter when you get to heaven. Until then, I recommend you ask the Holy Spirit to help this settle in your heart and believe it!

A Butterfly Illustration And Battle Instructions

Why is this so important? Consider this example:

---

[24] Don't be so surprised that God says we share His good nature. His plan for us from the beginning has been that we would be "in His image" and share "His likeness." See the appendix on the first mention of mankind.

A butterfly that still thinks it is a caterpillar will never fly.

In the same way, if we think our inner nature is to sin, we will always be "grounded" when it comes to living out what God has done in us.

If you have ever prayed: "not my will but Yours be done," or "let Your will be done in me," then be encouraged; He answered that prayer! More than anything else, you now want what God wants. You have been reborn to fly.

One challenge that many people have with this command is that it can seem like we are being told to live in *denial* of what we feel and want as normal imperfect people. Be careful here that the enemy does not deceive you into disobedience in favor of being "real." The Romans 6:11 way of thinking about ourselves is not at all about being in denial of, or ignoring, the feelings and ungodly impulses that we all still wrestle with. Just the opposite is true! This way of life is 100% authentic. Imagine the freedom of this kind of approach:

- We carefully acknowledge when we "feel like" doing something we know we shouldn't do.
- But then we remind ourselves that the "new me"—the new real me—doesn't truly want that.
- We conclude that "what I really want is to please and obey God."

Again, Paul doesn't say to "bury our head in the sand" when we don't feel like doing what God asks, or to pretend we don't feel that way. Instead we take bold action within ourselves to be **real** about the conflict within us. It is a fierce battle!

> I absolutely will not allow the world, the enemy, or my flesh to dictate to me what I conclude that I want.

I will not be a slave to the temporal impulses of sin! I am dead to sin; and I am profoundly and powerfully alive to God. So are you! Let's fight together to stay convinced that we want what God wants, despite what we might feel.

The Christian life is not about making ourselves stop doing the bad things we really want to do. It's not about forcing ourselves to do the *loathsome* things that we *should* do. It is about discovering the God who is so good that He changes who we are and what we want. A crucial command of the Christian life is to *defend the delights of our heart* by faith—faith in what He has done, what He sees in us, and who we are now.

Some Specifics Of What We Want And What We Don't Want

I can think of nothing in my many years of being a Christian that has helped me more in the battle against sin than being able to confidently say: *I don't want that; I want God and His plan for me more.*

- I don't want to eat too much or drink in excess.

    I want to take care of the body God has given me so I can serve Him and enjoy good health.

- That house that I don't need, or that car that I don't need, seem very appealing!

    But what I really want is the financial peace and freedom that God wants for me.

- Good try, devil, but NO! I do not want to look at that other woman that way.

    God has given me someone much better: my wife!

- Lord, it sure would be nice to have that money we gave to the church back in my account.

> *But what I really want is Your blessing on our family and finances. What I really want is to make an investment that impacts people for eternity. So I'm glad to give!*

To be very transparent and honest, on some days it takes a tremendous amount of faith to believe these types of things. Keep reading because chapter seven explains some powerful evidence that proves with even more certainty that we are dead to sin and alive to God.

In conclusion, I propose to you what I think Paul and Peter are both saying:

> In almost every case, you will end up doing **what you <u>perceive</u> you want to do**.

So you had better get in the battle to fight for your perception of what you really want. I guarantee you that the enemy is doing everything he can to influence "what you think you want."

Questions To Ponder

- Do you believe that you are dead to the power of sin and alive to the will of God?

- Do you believe that the commands of God are what you really want to do now, because of the new heart He has given you?

- Are you convinced that the opposing desires you may still feel are just the enemy's "smoke and mirror" tricks, destined to fade because of your friendship with God?

If not, make the decision to believe it today, and ask God for help. Just because it's true, doesn't mean it's easy!

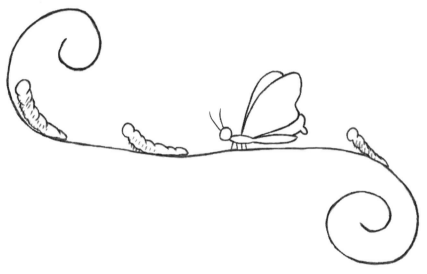

Why would a butterfly, who thinks he is still a caterpillar,
Ever expect to fly—or even try?

CHAPTER 6
STUDY AND APPLICATION GUIDE

Based on the sacrifice of Jesus Christ for us and the work of the Spirit of God within us, what is fundamentally different about us now that we have received the Truth of God?

    I was _____ to God and alive (inclined) to _____.
    But now I am dead to _____, and alive to _____ in Christ Jesus.

What is it that we are carefully instructed to believe about ourselves—what new perspective am I supposed to battle for?

Logizomai. God has made His notes—He's updated His "log" on you and me. He's come to a new conclusion about us, just as He did with Abraham. He's still looking at our heart—the deepest part of us—just as He always has. He's not ignoring the habits of our mind, will, or emotions, but those have never been of primary interest to Him anyway. He's looking at the core of us, and He sees His Son Jesus alive there! God does not have "blinders" on; He's not deceived about us.

Have you made the choice to believe that what God sees in you is what is really there?

Are you battling to believe that what God says of you is true?

What are some areas in your life where you need to go to war for what you perceive that you really want?

CHAPTER 7

How Could This Be True Of Me?
What Genuine Struggle with Sin Reveals

> "…the one who wants to do good. For I joyfully concur with the law of God in the inner man…"
> —Romans 7:21

Wrestling With Reality: When Faith Seems To Conflict With Fact

Is anyone thinking:

> How could this possibly be true of me?

I have certainly wondered:

> How could I be alive to God and dead to sin in light of my behavior and what goes on inside me?

Shouldn't we be able to look at the outward fruit of our lives and have a good idea of the reality inside of us? Romans 6 does not seem to add up.

Paul could relate to this same tension. He addresses these concerns in detail in Romans 7. My prayer is that you are as encouraged as I am about his conclusion:

Our agony when we fail in sin, and our genuine frustration in the battle to obey God, prove something amazing about us and God's work within us.

Provoked: What Is Pushing Our Buttons?

In the first half of Romans 7 Paul describes the effect of the law of God on us before we believed in Him. He explains that when we "suppressed the Truth" of God's good heart toward us, the law provoked rebellion within us by giving sin an opportunity. The good law of God revealed the corrupt perception we had of Him by igniting the desire to disobey.

Think of every children's cartoon you've ever seen that involved a **big red button** that said:

"Do Not Push."

What did you know was going to happen as soon as you saw that button on the screen? You knew it would get pushed, of course! Simply seeing the words on the button provoked a powerful desire within the cartoon character to do the opposite of what it says. Paul explains that the exact same thing happened when we encountered the commands of God. Of course we broke the "Thou Shalt Nots"; we didn't trust the motive of the Command Giver. When the motive of leadership is "suspect," obedience is not only undesirable, it is also often illogical. It feels overwhelmingly like "thin ice"—the opposite of what we want. Why obey someone who does not have my best interests at heart?

What The Conflict Within Christians Confirms

Notice Paul's careful description of the profound contrast now; something completely different is happening within us, even though our outward behavior may not have changed much yet:

> "...For I am not practicing what I would like to, but I am doing that very thing that I hate. But if I do the very thing that I do not want to do, I agree with the law, that it is good... For I know that nothing good dwells in me, that is, in my flesh... I find then the principle that evil is present in me, <u>the one who wants to do good</u>. For I joyfully concur with the law of God in the inner man." Romans 7:15-22[25]

In the 2nd half of Romans 7, Paul describes a part of the Christian experience that can be considered a "Walking Civil War." The physical shell that we live in is opposed to our true nature—the nature that is alive to God and loves Him. There is a battle raging within us between our fleshy body, which is still corrupted by sin, and our new inner nature that delights in the goodness of God.

Don't miss the main point that Paul makes in the "still doing what I don't want to do" passage:

> The fact that we so thoroughly despise the remaining sin in our lives **proves** that our hearts have been changed.

How could we want to change our behavior so badly if the nature of our hearts had not already been reborn? The genuine agony over our failures in the outward battle is evidence that God has already won the ultimate victory within us. If we were not already changed we would not care about ongoing sin.

What Trees Can Tell Us: It Takes Time

Our fleshy bodies are like a huge old tree that has died. Have you ever noticed how long the dead growth can linger after the tree actually died? Years! A new seed of Truth has been planted in the soil of our lives, but the old corrupt growth from years of deception is still hanging around.

---

[25] The NIV version of 7:22 is excellent as well: "For in my inner being I delight in God's law..."

It doesn't decompose overnight. This is why the outward appearance of our lives may not be reflecting the new inward reality of what God has done within us yet. It takes time for the new growth to show.

God changed everything when Christ proved for eternity His good heart toward us on the cross. Our old corrupt perception of Him was obliterated, and the old person with the rebellious inner nature died. A new person, who is alive to God, now lives. The old dead tree still lingers, but its days are numbered. Since God has made the Root new, He will also establish the new Shoot, and then the new Fruit. If a new plant is growing from a new root (Truth, not deception), *shouldn't we expect to see a new shoot (new desires)* **before** *we see new fruit (new behaviors)?*

Again, the new growth process takes time. But the butterfly will fly. The image forged in the dark room will one day be displayed for all to see. The faith God saw—and credited to you as righteousness—when you first believed will one day be seen by many others. How things have been (in reference to your behavior) is not how they will always be. You are alive to God; sin has already lost. You will see, and you won't be the only one!

Harness The Heartache From UnHealthy Habits

Understanding what my outward battle with sin confirms about the inner change in me has helped me on some dark days. Some habits are hard to kick. Many stumps of sin are not easily uprooted. But one of the main schemes the enemy used to keep dead sin anchored in my life was to **deceive** me into thinking that *what I do defines who I am*. Instead, the Spirit of God reminds me:

> God made you new, Jeremy, inclined to love and obey Him. If you fall into sin again, the emptiness, or frustration, or remorse, or anger, or disgust you feel can be a reminder that the real you could never be content in sin. Sinning does not make you a sinner by nature; your desire to change reveals your new nature.

The devil cannot keep me bound in sinful habits once I see myself differently. My regret when I do sin only reinforces what the Word of God tells me: that's not who I am any longer... and it's not what I want.

Knowing this can help you too. When you feel convicted, discouraged, remorseful, hopeless, trapped, disturbed by sin in your life, throw it back in the devil's face! Deeper than any desire for sin within you is a heart with a nature to be 100% for God. Remind the enemy of this when he attacks you about your habits. Thank God that the heartache you feel is evidence of the work He has already done (7:21-22); and praise Him for the promise to finish the work He began.[26]

Do you hate the sin that still plagues your life? Don't wonder if God has worked within you. Your hatred for your sin is the proof you need to believe... believe the new you is alive to Him.

Who wants to push the button?
(Trick question ☺)

---

[26] Philippians 1:6 (paraphrase) – For He who began a good work in you will continue maturing it until the day of Christ Jesus.

CHAPTER 7
Study And Application Guide

For this chapter's study guide, if you haven't been reading the full chapters in Romans, please go back and read chapters six and seven. They complement each other well.

In addition to that, let's reflect on a few Old Testament passages about the heart and its desires:

Deuteronomy 5:29

> "Oh that they had such a heart in them, that they would fear Me and keep all My commandments always, that it may be well with them and with their sons forever!"

Don't get hung up on the word "fear." It has much more to do with *honor* and considering God *supremely important* than it has to do with terror or dread. The terror part really only comes in when someone has made themselves His enemy and threatens His beloved children.

Notice here that in the same chapter where God gives the 10 commandments—in almost the same breath as the ominous "thou shalt nots"—we see that His heart was not to demand *white knuckle* obedience. He has never wanted outward obedience without the heart behind it. He has always been longing and planning to capture our hearts—to make them inclined toward His own. He has always desired to change our hearts so that our children and families would be blessed for generations. The gospel is the story of Christ finishing that work within us.

Reflect on that for a moment before you move on.

Psalm 37:4

> "Delight yourself in the LorD;
>
> And He will give you the desires of your heart."

When we are setting our hearts on God, then He will absolutely give us what we want. Why? Because the #1 One thing we are wanting then is God Himself!

When we face those Romans 7 moments, where our wretched habits don't line up, what we focus on is critical. Will we focus on our failures, our history, or our own inadequate efforts to change? Or will we delight ourselves in the incredible goodness of God?

Let's put our confidence in what He has done to make our hearts new; then our habits will follow.

Proverbs 4:23 (NIV)

> "Above all else, guard your heart, for everything you do flows from it."

This must be of critical importance if we are to prioritize it "above all else." God certainly makes looking at the heart and dealing with the heart His priority!

What do you think it means to guard your own heart? Does it mean to stay isolated, always play it safe, and make sure you never get hurt? (No!) Write your own description of this #1 priority.

Jeremiah 31:33-34

> "This is the covenant I will make with the people… (declares the Lord)
>
> I will put my law in their minds and write it on their hearts.
>
> I will be their God, and they will be My people…
>
> …they will all know Me…
>
> For I will forgive their wickedness
>
> And will remember their sins no more."

What is the new covenant? What does it have to do with God changing our hearts?

Do you see how God's plan and promise to us, since before Jesus was even born, was to give us new hearts that "joyfully concur with His law"? It has all been set up so that our "inner being would delight in His law."

I propose a new approach to the term "discipline" for you to consider:

> What if successful discipline is not about "white knuckle" stubborn determination to *make ourselves do the loathsome things we "should" do*?
>
> What if long-term change does not come from *forcing ourselves to stop doing the sinful things we "desire"*?

What if real discipline is about deciding what we really want beforehand, and then refusing to let fluctuating emotions and instant impulses from our flesh convince us otherwise?

God has given you a new heart with new desires. Trust in His work within you first. Indulge in the wonder of His goodness and His desires. Then your habits will change.

CHAPTER 8

Can We Have A Summary Of The "Good" News?
Our "Good" Redefined

> "…God causes all things to work together for the good of those who love Him… for (those) to be conformed to the image of His Son… What then? …If God is for us…
> —Romans 8:28-31

If We Knew What Is Good For Us

> "…God causes all things to work together for the good of those who love Him…" (8:28)

These are some of the most frequently quoted words in the Bible. But do we have in mind what God has in mind when we count on God to "work all things for our *good*"? I think many Christians get themselves in trouble because they have a different definition of what is "good for them" than God. So we often move forward believing that God will work everything for our "good," by our own definition, and then encounter hardship, loss, disappointment, suffering, betrayal, unfaithfulness, death, abuse, and dishonor. These things shake our faith because they look absolutely nothing like the "good" that we were expecting. If you have not experienced this yet, it is probably coming. I want to help you be prepared to weather the storm.

Paul explains clearly what God's definition of "our good" actually is in Romans 8. God knows exactly what is in our best interest at all times. It is not surprising that the definition lines up perfectly with the original intent that He had when He created us "in His image and likeness":[27]

"to be conformed to the **image** of His Son" (8:29)

"Our good" is to become more and more like Jesus Christ.[28] God is working all things together for this one simple goal. He has already won the battle to plant His image and nature within us. Now He is orchestrating history to shape our souls, character, and outward habits to be like Christ too. We are His plan to reach this lost world. If the world doesn't see Christ in us they may not see Him at all.

Hardships are still hard, but they can be a powerful catalyst to grow us into Jesus' good image. Loss shapes our perspective and can identify where our hearts are too attached to other things besides God. Disappointment can clear the cobwebs of worldly ambitions and refocus our hope on eternally significant goals. Suffering, betrayal, death of loved ones, anything we can experience—it may not be "good" in and of itself—but it can be used by God to shape us *for our good*. The dark room is where the image of Light, that is already deep in our spirit, is established within our souls. Sorrows may last the night, but joy comes in the morning.

What Image Do We Imagine? What Nature Is He Nurturing?

God is working all things for your good, and your good is to be continually made more thoroughly like Christ—into His image. This conclusion begs the questions: What is His image? What is He like?

---

[27] Genesis 1:26-27. See the appendix
[28] And the Son happens be "the radiance of (the Father's) glory, and the exact representation of His nature" (Hebrews 1:3). If we have seen the Son, we have seen the Father (John 14:8). They have the same image, the same likeness, the same nature.

My best advice is to get to know Him yourself. Spend time with Him. Share your life with Him in prayer and journaling. Listen to Him by reading His Word. Embrace the process God brings you through, although it will sometimes be very uncomfortable. Express both your joy and pain to God through praise and worship. See Him in others by being part of a church, especially in small group settings where you can safely ask questions. You will, of course, see Him by contrast sometimes in church, since the rest of us there are still being formed too. But the Spirit of God is able to show you the heart of God within imperfect people. That isn't too hard for Him!

Paul also gives us a glimpse of the image of God in this immediate context. It is easy to skip over these four simple words, but in my opinion they could be considered the conclusion and cornerstone of his entire Romans letter:

> "What then shall we say to these things? If **God is for us**, who is against us?" (8:31)

God is *for us*. He is for you. Paul does not simply say, "God *does* things for you." The scriptures say God **IS** for you. This is a profound conclusion about God's nature, His likeness, His image—not simply His actions.

It is the nature of God to be "for others." This is another way to say: God is love. Love lays down one's own life for His friends. We even see this within the trinity:

- the Son serves the Father and makes a dwelling place for the Spirit in His followers
- the Father exalts the Son and sends the Spirit to His people
- the Spirit reveals the Father and reminds His followers of everything the Son has said

So even within God Himself the "for Others" heart reigns. God has never had a selfish motive. He is perfectly selfless; He's 100% a promoter of others. That is good news for me and you!

How do I know this is correct and why am I confident that this is the most important Truth in all of history?

- First, <u>because of the cross</u>. This is the core message that is demonstrated by Christ on the cross. The only possible explanation for Christ accepting what He went through on the cross is that He is perfectly unselfish and 100% "for others."[29] Since He is the Son of God—the radiance of the Father's glory and the exact representation of the Father's nature—what does that prove about the Father? He is wholeheartedly "for us" too!

God is completely devoted to something; what do you think that is? (Be careful with your answer because it will shape just about everything in your life!) The cross proves that both the Son and the Father are passionate, undistracted, continually delighting in, and completely resolved to **bless and promote other people**.

- Second, I know this Truth is of critical importance <u>because this is the first thing the devil went after</u> in the garden of Eden. This is the central deception that caused the fall. Go back and read Genesis 3 and see if there is another good interpretation besides that the devil led Eve and Adam to sin by first *deceiving them with the perception that God was not "for them."*[30] The devil would not have been able to get them to **choose** sin if he did not first lead them to **desire** it. And they would not have desired to *push the big red disobedience button* if they had not first been **deceived** about God's motive behind the command.

- Third, <u>because of what we like most</u> and, in contrast, <u>what we despise most in others</u>. What do you despise most when you see it in others? Selfishness, pride, and conceit—when people put themselves before others and think of themselves as

---

[29] See also Chapter 3
[30] See also the appendix. You have read the appendix, right? ☺

more important than others. In contrast, what do you like and admire most in others? Unselfishness, humility, compassion: when people put others before themselves and think of others first.[31] We are wired to loathe selfishness and embrace humility.

SIMPLE SUMMARY

Here is a simple gospel summary; a huge part of appreciating "the" good news is that our "good" has been redefined:

- God is always working everything together for *our good*.
- *Our good* is to be conformed to the image of His Son.
- The image of His Son is a "for us"/"for others" image.

God is shaping us into this specific image, this likeness. He has defined *what is best for us* as being made into *for others* people—people who have an inward nature and outward way of life that reflects Him. God is loving us by making us the kind of people who care first about others. That means He is shaping us into people who serve others, build healthy relationships, and humbly lay down our lives to promote others. This is the nature He has planted within us, the desire He is cultivating in our souls, and the fruit of good works He has promised to harvest from us.

We are like a mirror reflecting an image—like the moon reflecting the light of the sun. My wife is not only an incredible example of this herself, but she has a great explanation of it too:

She says, "Moon Jesus!" (with a big smile!)

More specifically: "Be a moon for Jesus; reflect the light of the Son."

---

[31] See Philippians 2. I hope to have the opportunity to write about this chapter one day soon. It is my favorite.

Some "Essential" Conclusions

I can think of a few essential beliefs that have been etched within me from the Scriptures and that I have vowed to no longer doubt:

- God exists
- His Word is 100% True and alive
- The way we know God is through Christ
- God will always provide what I need to please Him and do what He has asked me to do

But no core belief has anchored me in my walk with God as firmly as this one:

- No matter what happens, or what I feel, **God is for me—He always has my best interests at heart**

I would need a much longer book to recount how many times God has sustained me in struggles by reminding me that **He is for me**.

It's time for you to draw the line in the sand too. Settle this issue once and for all today:

- What do you believe about God's unchanging nature, and will you allow your perspective of God to be defined by past assumptions or ever-changing circumstances and emotions?

- Where does your heart and mind go when life gets hard and pain overwhelms you?

- Have you decided to trust His perfectly good and unselfish motives no matter what?

- Have you resolved to function with the assumption that He has your best interests in mind, even when your mind can't understand, and your emotions are screaming, "There's no way that is possible!"?

o   Have you resolved to trust Him—to believe that the eternal fruit He is working to produce within you is worth the temporary pain and sacrifice you are being asked to endure today?

In His infinite wisdom and power, God is working to establish this faith within you—to help you believe. He is perfectly "for you" and your brothers and sisters in this one faith. He is shaping you into this same "for others" image, so you are not alone in the battle to believe. But, you must choose to accept the gift He is offering.

Once you Accept, you're already changed (and God sees it) (chapter 4).

Then you Expect, and the new you starts to break through (chapter 5)

Then you Connect: I'm not who I was. God has given me a new heart like His! (chapter 6)

Reflecting the Light of the Son...
Sounds "Good" to me!

CHAPTER 8
STUDY AND APPLICATION GUIDE

Before you read this chapter in Gospel Boot Camp, how would you have described what is "good" for you and the people you care for most?

How may your outlook be changing based on the chapter—and especially the Romans 8 text?

Does it seem awkward to think of God as being absolutely "for others"? What other agendas, or competing purposes, have you pictured Him pursuing?

What are some specific areas where God is shaping you to be more like Him, in the sense of being "others before self"?

Would you say that you are resisting the transformation process or resolved to fight fiercely in the battle to believe?

CHAPTER 9

WHAT SHOULD MY GOAL AND STRATEGY BE?
THE CHRISTIAN MISSION, VISION, AND JOB DESCRIPTION

> "...offer your bodies as a living sacrifice... be transformed
> by the renewing of your mind, so that you may
> demonstrate what the will of God is...do not think more
> highly of yourself than you ought to think ..."
> —Romans 12:1-3

"WHAT I AM HERE FOR" IS NOT ABOUT ME

What is the purpose and mission that God entrusted to you for the rest of your time on earth? And what is the plan for fulfilling it? As we approach the end of this book I want to encourage you with a clear goal and strategy. Let's allow God's word to shape our assumptions and perception once again.

There is a prevailing idea in our American church culture that we all have our own separate purpose and destiny. Everyone is *respectfully* gathering as many resources and as much support for their "Godly calling" as possible, hopefully without infringing too rudely on the ambitions of others. I have often felt like I am walking a delicate "fine line" with my efforts to serve God as a Christian. I must "finish the work God has given me," but I find myself often serving someone else's vision. I volunteer, contribute, and commit to the God-dreams of others, but I need more help with mine. I don't want to intrude on the plans of my brothers, or abandon the vision of my pastors, but what about me? God has a plan for me, and I don't want to miss it.

Paul turns this whole perspective upside down, freeing us from the trap of selfish ambition and the prison of what-about-me thinking in Romans 12:1-3:

> "...in view of God's mercy... offer your bodies as a living sacrifice... be transformed by the renewing of your mind, so that you may prove what the will of God is... do not think more highly of yourself than you ought to think, since God has distributed to each a measure of faith."

The response God desires from us is for us to be *living sacrifices*. We become the offering. In contrast to what culture teaches us, we all have the same ultimate purpose and mission: we are carrying on Christ's work of demonstrating the heart of God to the world.[32] Christ has passed us the baton of *reaching the world with God's love*. When we offer our lives to God we become part of the proof the world needs to be able to know God themselves. Christ's sacrifice sustains us when God is on trial in the courtroom of our hearts; now God asks us to be living sacrifices so the world has present-day evidence to help them as they render their own verdict. We are a crucial part of His plan to give the world hope, faith, and life. Now we are the demonstration of His righteousness, alongside Christ.

In light of this purpose and mission, we should not be competing for resources and support. We are here to reveal a loving, for-others God. So we must be generous. When I use my resources to help you in your calling, I am fulfilling mine. That IS my calling. I accomplish the work God has given me by living with a "for others" heart, one that gives, serves, and promotes other people. Our focus must shift to "Him and them"; it can't be on me.

---

[32] See Chapter 3 on Romans 3

The "Good Life" is a life that is Given Away

Consider Niagara Falls and the Dead Sea. Think of how much power and life flows through Niagara; but at the Dead Sea everything is stagnant. At Niagara, everything is green and nourished; at the Dead Sea everything is barren and starved. What is the difference? Niagara is 100% poured out; at the Dead Sea nothing goes out. At Niagara, whatever comes in is freely released; at the Dead Sea everything that flows in is trapped and hoarded.

The "good life" that God has in mind for us is like Niagara. If we are poured out and offered up as living sacrifices, then God's power will flow and His light will shine to bless those around us. But if we hold too tight, live for ourselves, and "look out for #1," God's power will be restricted and our lives will be defined by stagnant darkness. Our job as Christians is not to accomplish great things for God in the world by our own strength and ingenuity, but to be fully surrendered to Him in faith so He can be great within us and through us. It's about the world seeing Him in us. When their tarnished "image" of God is confronted by the love they see in us, they can be transformed too.

How to Grow as a Generous Giver

How do we grow and make progress in this mission?

>Continually have our minds transformed (12:2).

Notice the 1st thinking transformation Paul lists:

>Not thinking too highly of self (12:3).

We must refuse to let our thinking be prideful and be careful of conceit in our perspective. Self-absorbed thinking—being defined in our own minds by past failure, or even worldly success—either one can be spiritually deadly. I can even get off track when I am too consumed with the work God has done in me alone.

The power to grow is unleashed when we recognize that God has done something incredible not only in ourselves, but also in others. He has given everyone in His church a "measure of faith" (12:3). He has entrusted each brother and sister in the faith with a new heart and calling that destines them for tremendous eternal purpose. They may be struggling just like we are with doing what they don't want to do (Ch. 7); but that is proof of God's work in them too. They are dead to sin and alive to God just like me and you (Ch. 6)! We praise God best when we celebrate His work in others. We are most successful in fulfilling our calling when we find ways to help others accomplish theirs.

What is the best way to grow in my own calling and be effective in the work God has given me?

> Answer: See the potential in others, and offer what I have to promote them.

Our Conclusion—A Simple Goal And Strategy

> Be "for others." Embody the nature of God.

You are already dead to sin and alive to God because of His work of grace in your life. Now offer yourself fully to Him so He can accomplish His will to bless others through you. Embrace the process of transformation into the image of Christ. He is the way; He is the life; He is the good that God has in mind for you.

When you think of what Christ has done for you, what does that lead you to want to do for someone else?

Spend some time reflecting on that. Talk to your friends in church, a mentor, or a pastor about that. Share with them about the light of Christ that you see in them, and ask God to help them recognize His life in you.

Say no to "Dead Sea" / "No Outlet" living;
Aim for "Niagra:" it is most blessed to give what we receive.

CHAPTER 9
STUDY AND APPLICATION GUIDE

SPIRITUAL GIFTS ASSESSMENT

Ask someone in leadership at your church to recommend a spiritual gifts assessment guide. These can be found online as well, and I plan to make one available on Gospel Boot Camp website.

Use the guide to learn about you own gifts, but don't stop there. Ask a few friends to take the assessment too. Share your results and pray together for wisdom to encourage and support each other.

CHAPTER 10
WHAT IS THE HEART BEHIND IT ALL?
HAVING A HEART THAT HONORS HEAVEN

> "...Christ has become a Servant..."
> —Romans 15:8

Close your eyes and picture God for a moment…

What do you see? How do you imagine Him to be?

If our lives are following the path through Romans in response to the Righteousness of God:

from Rejection	(Chapters 1-3)
to Revelation	(Chapters 3-8)
to Resistance/Restoration	(Chapters 9-11)
to Reflection	(Chapters 12-16)

…then **what image are we aiming to reflect?**

Some see…	But we know…
A Harsh Judge	A Gentle Savior who defends us

Too much Impersonal Wrath	One who, in profound compassion, took personal responsibility for the punishment we deserved
A god who seems Distant	A Good Shepherd who came to us and is still with us every day
An Unconcerned god of Apathy	A loving Father whose very essence is to be captivated with blessing His own children
An Enabling god of Infinite Handouts	A real Friend who is willing to hold us accountable to grow, even if that means some "tough love"
A Proud, Self-serving Dictator	A Humble, Servant-hearted King, whose greatest delight is to use all His power and wisdom to love and serve His people

What image of God is etched on your heart? How would you describe Him?

What does a life that profoundly glorifies God really look like?

What is the practical picture that reveals our "for others" God?

Jesus! This is the answer that my kids always jokingly give whenever I ask them some deep, philosophical, churchy question that they aren't in the mood to really think about. (I am sure you have *never* felt that way as you read through this book—no, not for a moment!)

My kids just answer: "Jesus." How can I disagree with them, or improve on that?

(Pray for my kids, please! They need it because their dad is off-the-deep-end about the things of God, and He still has plenty of work to do on me.)

Hopefully, Jesus is the one we picture when we close our eyes and picture God. He is the only Way to the Father, the One Truth that is the essence of the Father, the only Life that is one with the Father; no one comes to the Father except through Jesus Christ. Jesus is the radiance of the Father's glory and the exact representation of His Nature—Jesus is **the** Image of the incorruptible God. Jesus' life is the perfect Revelation of the Righteousness of God.

> "For I tell you that **Christ has become a <u>Servant</u> of the Jews on behalf of God's Truth**, so that the promises... might be confirmed, and... that the Gentiles might glorify God for His mercy..." — Romans 15:8-9

I propose that we include the term "Servant" very high on our list of *words to describe God*. When Jesus came to reveal God to a deceived and corrupted world, He came as a servant. His example of serving is not simply a picture of what He wants us to make sure our lives look like; serving is a picture of God's own heart. When He expects compassion, selflessness, patience, sacrifice He is only looking for the same thing He originally created us for: to bear the true likeness of Our God.

When He asks us to deny ourselves, take up our cross, and follow Him, He isn't asking us to do any more than He has already done, to give more than He has given, or to be more humble than He has always been. His call is a simple invitation to join Him in the joy of living for others instead of for ourselves. God knows the "for others" life is the one that will be most satisfying, meaningful, rewarding, and eternally significant for us. It truly is an honor and privilege to serve.

Specific Servant-Centered Scriptures

If we are resolved to reflect His true likeness, then we must become servants of others. Go back to Romans and read chapters 12 through 15; God's humble heart that puts others before self is almost oozing off the pages!

Romans 12:

> And do not be conformed to this world, but be transformed by the renewing of your mind, so that you may prove what the will of God is, that which is good and acceptable and perfect. For through the grace given to me I say to everyone among you not to think more highly of himself than he ought to think; but to think so as to have sound judgment, as God has allotted to each a measure of faith. (verses 2-3)

> Be devoted to one another in brotherly love; give preference to one another in honor (verse 10)

> Bless those who persecute you; bless and do not curse. (verse 14)

> Be of the same mind toward one another; do not be haughty in mind, but associate with the lowly. (verse 16)

Romans 13:

> For because of this you also pay taxes, for rulers are servants of God, devoting themselves to this very thing. (verse 6)

> For this, "You shall not commit adultery, You shall not murder, You shall not steal, You shall not covet," and if there is any other commandment, it is summed up in this saying, "You shall love your neighbor as yourself." Love does no wrong to a neighbor; therefore love is the fulfillment of the law. (verses 9-10)

But put on the Lord Jesus Christ, and make no provision for the flesh in regard to its lusts. (verse 14)

Romans 14:

Now accept the one who is weak in faith, but not for the purpose of passing judgment on his opinions. (verse 1)

For not one of us lives for himself, and not one dies for himself; for if we live, we live for the Lord, or if we die, we die for the Lord; therefore whether we live or die, we are the Lord's. (verses 7-8)

Therefore let us not judge one another anymore, but rather determine this—not to put an obstacle or a stumbling block in a brother's way. (verse 13)

For if because of food your brother is hurt, you are no longer walking according to love. Do not destroy with your food him for whom Christ died. (verse 15)

So then we pursue the things which make for peace and the building up of one another. (verse 19)

It is good not to eat meat or to drink wine, or to do anything by which your brother stumbles. (verse 21)

Romans 15:

Now we who are strong ought to bear the weaknesses of those without strength and not just please ourselves. Each of us is to please his neighbor for his good, to his edification. For even Christ did not please Himself; but as it is written, "The reproaches of those who reproached You fell on Me." (verses 1-3)

Therefore, accept one another, just as Christ also accepted us to the glory of God. (verse 7)

As I bring this book to a close, I hope you have come to appreciate that being a good follower of Christ is not about keeping the right set of rules. In the same way that the new soldier (from the introduction) can't simply be given a daily task list from his commanding officer that applies every day and in all situations, being a genuine believer is much more than a simple list of "dos and don'ts." Reflect back on Paul's central idea in Romans:

> "(The gospel) is the power of God for salvation to all who believe… because in it the righteousness of God is revealed, from faith to (ever increasing) faith…" —Romans 1:16-17

As I have explored the gospel with you in this book, what I pray I have presented well is a clear and accurate picture of Who God really is, What He is like, and a simple way of approaching life that will help us walk closely with Him. Our God is a servant-hearted Person. All the power of the gospel to save, transform, and sustain us comes from the revelation of His goodness. He invites us to be like Him; bearing His image has always been His plan for us, and good options to live this out are unlimited!

A Soul that Lives Worthy of the Gospel must First be Touched by It

I plan to continue with this same goal of helping us *picture God well* so we can walk closely with Him in my next book project. Would you pray for me as I plan to tackle Philippians 2 next? A quick paraphrase preview of that content fits perfectly here in our conclusion:

> I ask of you only one thing: that you conduct yourselves in a manner that is worthy of the gospel. This means standing firm in one spirit with each other—with one mind striving together for the faith of the gospel.
>
> Let the encouragement, consolation, fellowship, affection, and compassion that Christ has poured out you lead you to make my joy complete by uniting you in this one mind, spirit, and purpose:

Gospel Bootcamp

> Do nothing from selfishness or prideful conceit, but with humility of mind consider one another to be more important than yourselves. Don't fix your attention on your own personal interests; look out for the interests of others.

This attitude I've just described—this outlook—this approach to life—this is the one to have within yourselves! It's the same one that was in Christ Jesus:

His outward form was the perfect representation of the inward nature of God.

> In His thinking, He did not equate God with "grasping"—as in grasping for Himself. Instead, He emptied Himself; He took on the form of a servant—He was made a man.

> Even more, as man, what was He found doing? He humbled Himself by being obedient to the point of death—even death on a cross.

> This is why God exalted Him—because He lived authentically with this one, humble, gospel-worthy mindset.

> —Philippians 1:27 – 2:11

Let's make this kind of gospel-worthy life our ambition too.

WHERE THE RUBBER MEETS THE ROAD

Who are the people in your life that are difficult to love? Write down a list of at least two...

Jeremy Weimer

Share honestly with God in prayer how you feel toward them…

Ask Him to help you love them as He first loved you—

    To see them with eyes of understanding and compassion
    To value them despite their imperfections and difficulties

APPENDIX

The Law Of 1ˢᵀ Mention Of Mankind
Specific Purpose and Seeds Planted

"after their kind... with seeds in them... in His Image..."
—Genesis 1 – 3

Let's look at the Creation and Fall of Man stories from a simple and reliable Bible interpretation perspective:

Notice **summary statements**; in many cases the Bible interprets itself for us.

Look for **what is repeated**; that will tell us what is important.

Notice the **pattern and structure of the text**; this will identify what should be compared and contrasted.

We know from the *summary statements* in Genesis 1:26-27 that God's original intent for mankind is that we would be *"in His image"—that we would bear His image and reflect His likeness.* This one specific eternal purpose is why every human life has so much value and why each of us has so much potential. Even as finite beings, we can honor an infinite God. In spite of our imperfections, the perfect nature of God can be seen in us. Every life matters, and no life is without hope or significance.

There is also a very clear **repeated pattern** in the Genesis 1 creation story. Recognizing the pattern helps us better understand and appreciate the message and meaning of the story:

Day 1 (vs 3-5)	Day 4 (vs 14-19)
Light Light separated from darkness	Two great Lights to give Light To Light, govern, and separate the day and night

Day 2 (vs 6-8)	Day 5 (vs 20-23)
Expanse in Waters (Sky/heaven) Separated waters "above and below"	Living creatures in the Water and Sky Creatures "above and below" "after their kind" multiplying

Day 3 (vs 9-13)	Day 6 (vs 24-31)
Dry Land/earth Separated Earth and sea	Living creatures on the Land "after their kind" (x5) Cattle, creeping things, beasts on the Earth

Day 3 - PART 2	Day 6 - PART 2
PLANTS with seed (x4) bearing fruit (x3) after their kind Would multiply over the land	MAN in God's image (x3) and bearing His likeness (after His kind) Would rule and multiply over the rest of creation

The patterns charted here confirm that everything in the Genesis 1 story illustrates the concept from the summary statements. As the moon reflects the light of the sun, God's intent for us is that we would reflect His Light.[33] As the creatures multiply and fill the earth, mankind's purpose is to fill the earth with the glory of God (since wherever we go God intends

---

[33] Matthew 5:14-16—We are the light of the world. God's eternal purpose for us is that the world would see His goodness in us, that He would be glorified through us, that those in darkness would find the light because of us.

that we reflect His likeness). Just as every other living creature in the story is "after a certain kind," He intended for us to be "after **His** kind"—in other words, like Him in character and love.

There is also a clear connection, based on the pattern of the text, between the **plants and mankind**. The connection is often overlooked but it's critically important:

> The creations of day 4 complete the pattern of day 1 (sun and moon give light)
>
> The creations of day 5 complete the pattern of day 2 (fish and birds fill the waters and sky)
>
> The creations of day 6 complete the pattern of day 3 – but there are 2 parts
>
>> (Animals fill and "complete" the land, then we have *plants and mankind*)

What Is The Significance Of The Connection Between Plants And Mankind?

#1: Both bear a type of "fruit." Plants bear literal physical fruit. *Mankind bears spiritual fruit*; we are intended to bear the image of God by producing this fruit:

> "By this My Father is glorified, that you bear much fruit..." (John 15)
>
> "But the Fruit of the Spirit is: love, joy, peace, patience, kindness, goodness, faithfulness, gentleness, self-control..." (Galatians 5)

#2: Both plants and mankind have *"seed" that determines the type of plant that grows and the type of fruit produced*. The type of physical seed in a plant determines everything about the plant and the fruit it produces. It's exactly the same with mankind:

> The type of spiritual "seed" in us—the faith perspective and perception of God within us—will be the most significant factor that determines the type of lives we live and the fruit our lives produce.[34]

As long as the right type of "seed" is within us (the Truth of the Word of God, supported by a healthy relationship with God) we will fulfill our intended purpose and bear fruit that glorifies God. The seed influences:

- Our thoughts (so that we think like Him)
- Our hearts (so that our emotions and desires are like His)
- Our will (so that we choose His way)

But if the wrong type of seed takes root in our hearts, then we will bear a different kind of fruit. This is how the creation story connects with the fall of man story:

- In Genesis 1, we learn about God's intent for mankind and the important of the type of seed.

- In Genesis 2,[35] we see the command, and *the command tests the seed*. (If we know God, trust Him, and love Him—if the right seed is rooted in us—we will obey. If not, we won't.)

- In Genesis 3, we see the impact when corrupt seed takes root.

---

[34] Please forgive me the fruit / produce pun, and see Jesus' parables of seeds and soils in Matthew 13:1-52. Even Jesus said this "seed" concept is of critical foundational importance in Mark's rendering: "Don't you understand this parable? How will you understand any parable?" (Mark 4:13). This seed/perception of God concept I'm writing about it essential to understand the kingdom of God and how it operates.

[35] Genesis 2 is a story about rest, provision, and companionship for man/Adam because of God's faithfulness and generosity. Our ability to appreciate and enjoy these blessings depend on our trust and relationship with Him. So it is very fitting for the command that tests our trust to be found in the middle of this story.

ONE LITTLE "OR TOUCH IT" MAKES ALL THE DIFFERENCE

Notice that when the serpent first approached Eve in Genesis 3, while the True seed was in place within her, her initial response indicated she had no desire at all to disobey God's command and every desire to obey Him:

> She said that God said: "You will not eat from it, *or touch it*, or you will die." (3:3, italics added for emphasis)

What jumps out to me about this text, in comparison to the actual command from Gen 2:16, is that Eve added "or touch it." Did you notice the addition? It's important because it reflects something about Eve. Her words indicate that her thinking and desires are along these lines:

> "I don't want to be anywhere near disobedience to the God who is so good to me."

Can you sense how she is perfectly comfortable with the boundaries God had given? She was happy to keep a safe distance from disobedience; she trusted God. Her slightly modified rendering of the original command doesn't give any indication that she is struggling to obey. Quite the opposite! She is grateful for the word of warning and voluntarily going the extra mile to comply.

Now notice the stark contrast within Eve after the devil planted his seed of deception about God and His motives behind the command (3:6-7):

> "When the woman **saw**:
>   that the tree was good for food,
>   And that it was a delight to the eyes,
>   And that the tree was desirable to make one wise,
> She took from its fruit and ate; and she gave also to her husband with her, and he ate. The eyes of both of them were opened."

Did you see how did she went from *despising* disobedience to *desiring* disobedience?

How did breaking God's command change from being *unthinkable and foolish* to appearing *delightful and wise*?

Does the text say **when** she ate, **then** she saw?

Did the outward choice result in Eve's darkened perception, mind, and heart?

Not at all! In fact, the verse says the opposite. It says she "saw" first; then she "ate." This means sin was already taking root within Eve before the outward action took place. The devil had begun to corrupt her view of God with his lies. Then her outward choice happened and solidified the evil seed of sin within Eve. Her perspective of God had been corrupted first, when the serpent planted suspicion about God's motives. This transformed everything else within her and made her inclined to sin.

BACK TO BOOT CAMP, RETURNING TO ROMANS

Consider the story of the man on the frozen lake again. It deals with the exact same principals of false seed and corrupted perception as the Fall of Man story—but it's in reverse. Eve and Adam go from walking in the Truth to being lost in lies. The man on the lake was overcome by lies; then he was set free by the truth. Paul's explanations of mankind and the gospel throughout Romans depend on these same principles of seeds planted and perception.

Having this understanding of the original design of people, and the dynamics of sin, will be a tremendous help to us. We are in a battle to break free from both the enemy's lies and the influence of man-made religion; they form a powerful influence that pushes us to depend on ourselves to "do better" and keep a long list of rules. But this is the wrong type of seed to depend on. No matter how hard we may try, **we can't**

expect to consistently produce genuine delicious fruit from the seed of a thorn bush! Only the True seed can grow fruit that truly honors God. When we focus on appreciating what Jesus Christ has done to free us from sin's trap, we will find that a new root is established within us. That is when the fruit God has always wanted will naturally be produced.

There are two key questions that you and I need to ask ourselves:

1. Do I have a good grasp on the clear purpose that God has created me for? Have I grown to understand that my value is a person and to other people is based on whether my life reflects God and whether people see Christ through me?

2. What seed is planted in the "soil" that is me? What do my habits, thoughts, and desires reveal about the seed and perception of God that is rooted in me?

Isaiah 5:

> My beloved had a vineyard...
>
> He dug... removed its stones... planted it... built a tower... hewed a wine vat...
>
> Then He expected it to produce good grapes, but it produced only worthless ones.

Thanks be to God that because of Christ, this does not need to be the end of the story.